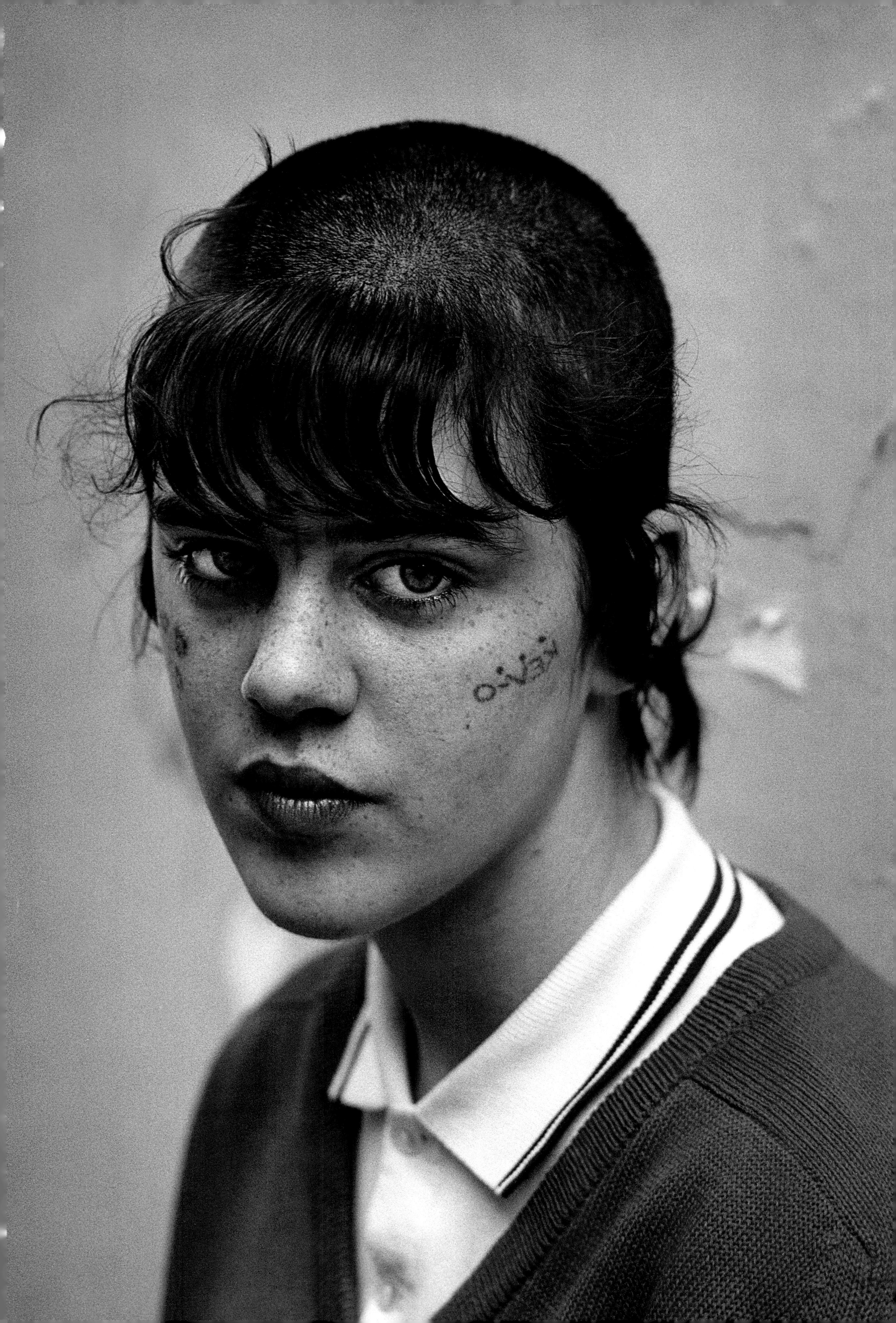

DEREK RIDGERS

THE LONDON YOUTH PORTRAITS

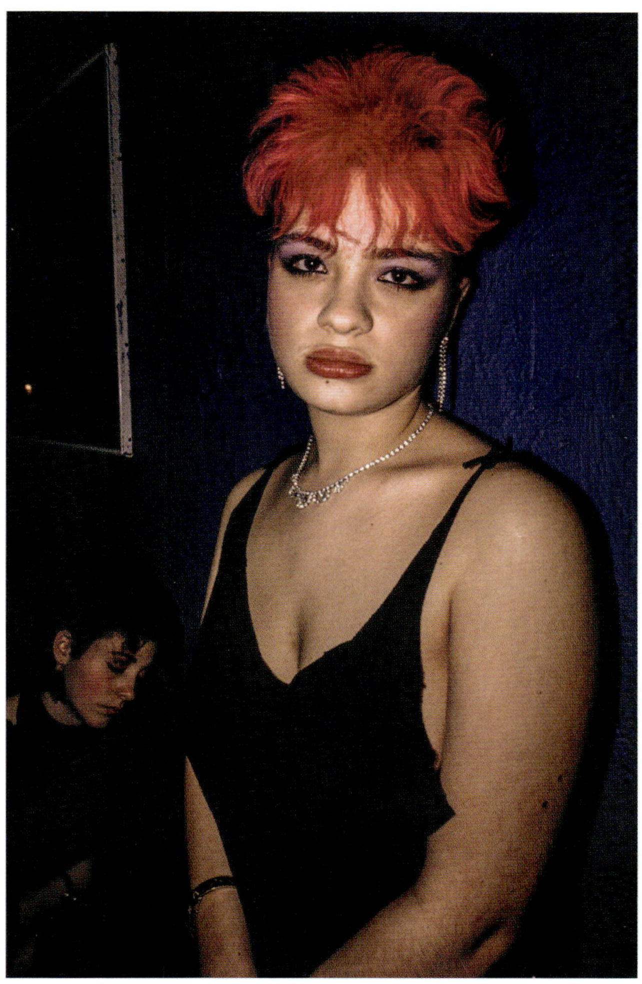

Foreword by Sean O'Hagan

ACC ART BOOKS

how we were then...

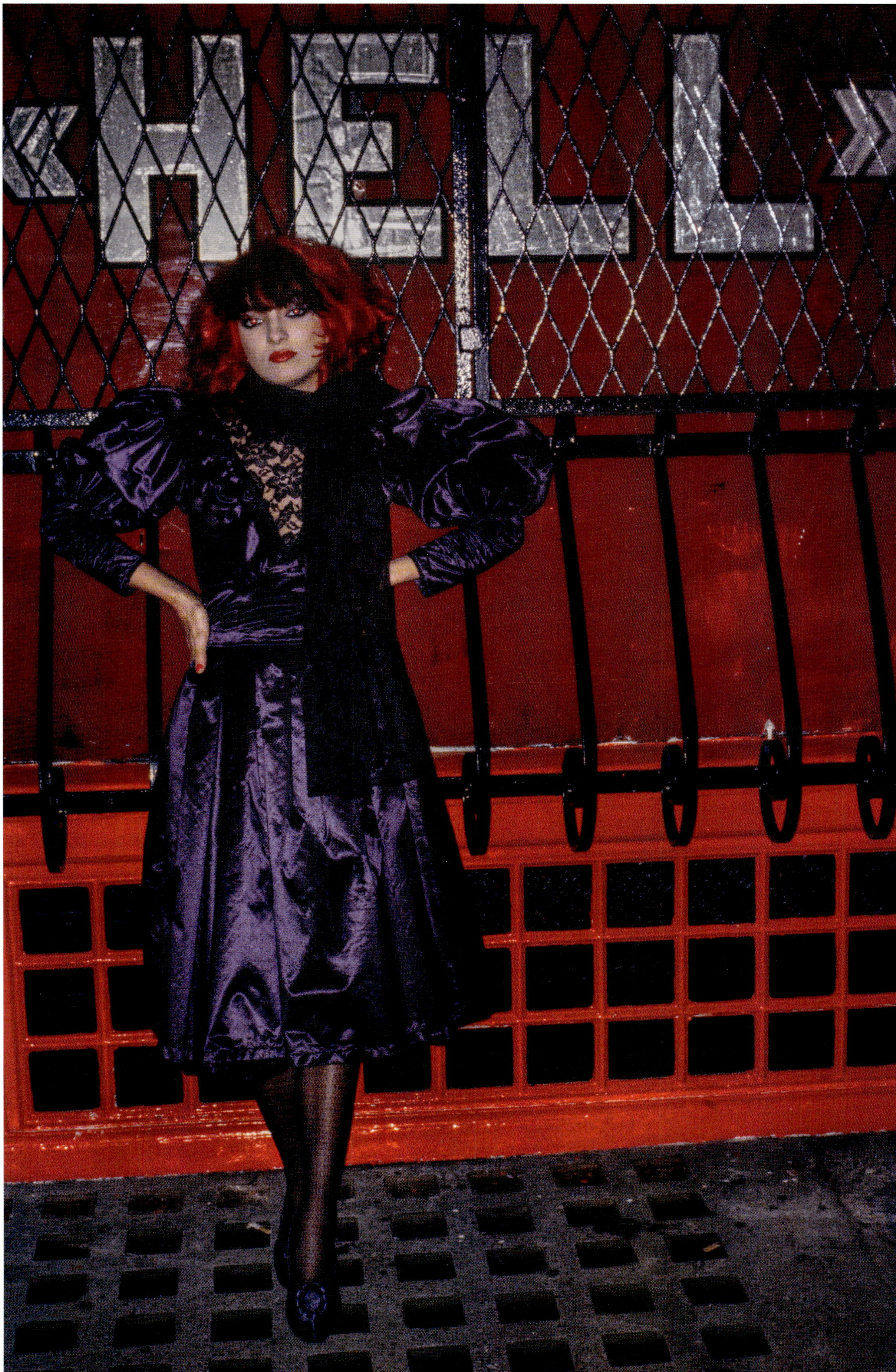
«HELL»

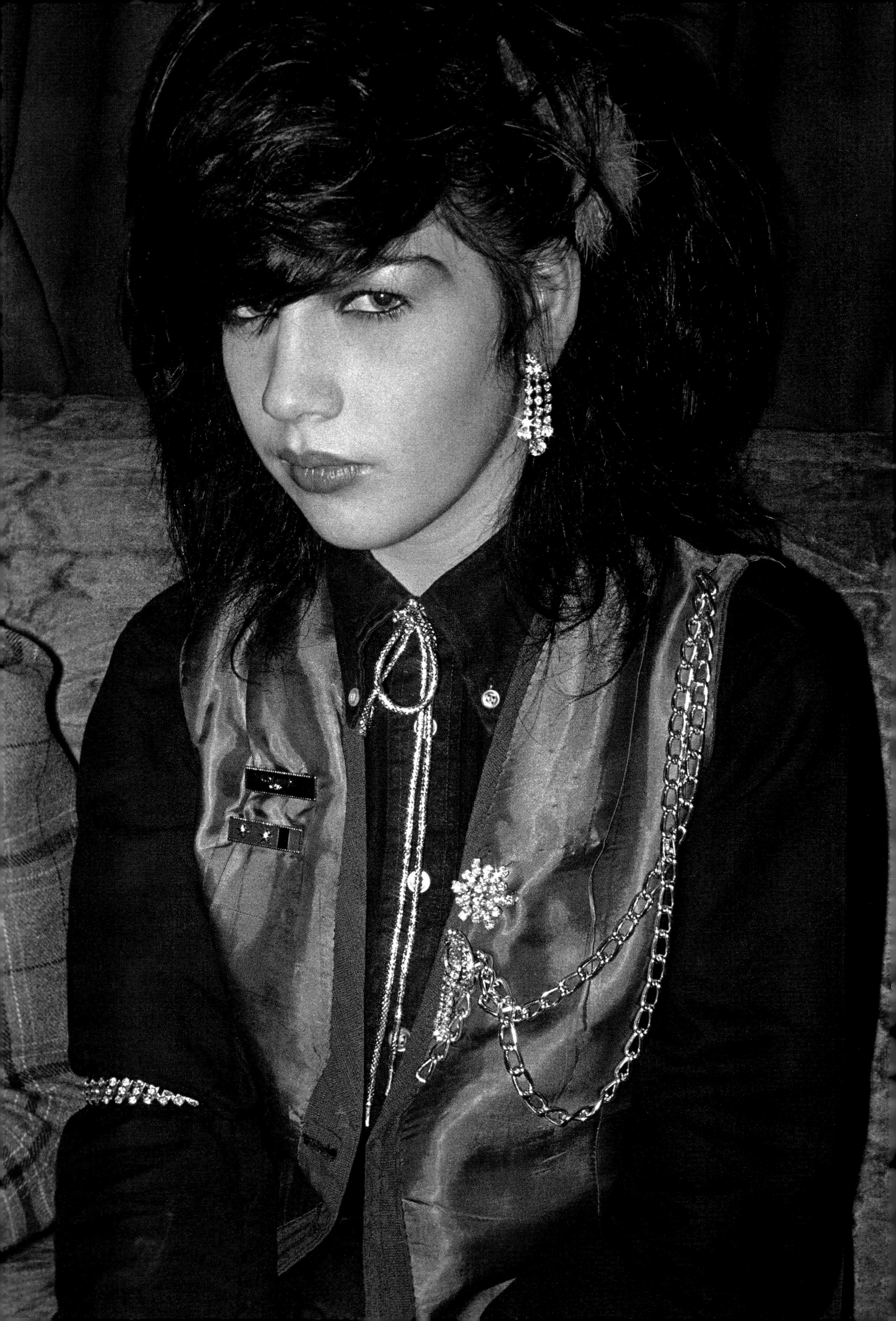

Derek Ridgers once described himself as 'one of life's observers, constantly on the margins with a camera'. It is perhaps unsurprising, then, that his outsider temperament led him to the more exotic individuals who flourished in London's nocturnal demi-monde from the late-1970s post-punk era to the more flamboyant club culture of the 1980s.

During that time, Ridgers tirelessly trawled the capital's streets, bars, clubs and after-hours drinking dens, photographing skinheads, punks, post-punks, new romantics, goths, fetishists and every hybrid style and subculture that emerged out of those tribal identities.

The capital's fast-changing, self-revitalising youth culture has been fertile territory for street and documentary photographers alike since the 1950s, when a young Ken Russell snapped teenagers doing the hand-jive in The Cat's Whisker coffee bar in Soho. In the ensuing decades, the focus of their attention tended to be one particular subcultural group, whether the surviving remnants of British Teddy Boy culture that Chris Steele Perkins observed in his 1979 book, *The Teds,* or the revealing glimpse of Britain's enduring skinhead culture that Nick Knight recorded in his 1982 book, *Skinhead.*

What sets Ridgers apart is his long-term dedication to the subject, a doggedness that borders on the obsessive. The striking portraits collected here are a mere fraction of the tens of thousands of images that make up his extensive and wide-ranging archive, which stretches back to shooting Bay City Rollers fans outside Hammersmith Odeon in June 1975.

This book's chronological starting point begins three years later. As the captions alone attest, the photographs herein amount to a visual record of London club culture in the decade that followed, from Billy's and Blitz in 1978 and '79, through Le Beat Route and The Batcave in the early 1980s and on to the likes of Taboo and Sacrosanct in the mid-to-late '80s. What immediately catches the eye is the clothes and the hairstyles, the efforts '80s clubbers made to dress up and stand out, whether the Batcave goths with their pale faces, dark eyes and artfully unruly hair or the more sexually indeterminate glam stylings of the extroverts at Taboo.

During that period, Ridgers also photographed individuals who caught his eye on the street and the results fall into two equally revealing categories: those that echo the extravagant style of the club portraits and those that conform to a more determinedly proletarian ideal of 'outsiderness', even social isolation, whether

Mel, Bowie Night at Billy's, Soho 1978.

Mohican-ed punks or hardcore skins. Ridgers was threatened more than once while photographing young skinheads and now describes his initial approach as 'extremely naive and a bit stupid'. It nevertheless resulted in some of his most starkly dramatic portraits – all those intense young men with cropped heads and cold stares. Here and there, too, particularly in his portraits of skinhead girls, there are softer, less sullen engagements with his camera; moments when his subject's beauty is made more apparent by their lack of any elaborate stylistic artifice.

Throughout the book, one can sense that Ridgers' compositional skill was honed by the very act of constantly taking pictures, the results becoming ever more intimate and revealing. He has spoken of the importance of being 'detached, even distant' from his subjects, a formal decision that conversely lends some of these portraits a curious intensity. It is most palpable in the penetrating and defiant stares of many of his skinhead subjects, for whom the camera is a mirror of their uber-masculinity. It is there, too, in a much more subtle and complex way, in his portraits of young men and women whose interactions with him are more tentative and uncertain. Lisa, a young woman he encountered on London's Shaftesbury Avenue in 1984, is a case in point. Her returned gaze is vulnerable, almost shy, despite her determinedly tough exterior – the cropped hair, dyed fringe, tattoo-ed face and Union Jack pin on the lapel of her Crombie. More striking still is Caroline, a young woman photographed at the fetish club Skin 2, who somehow exudes a rosy-cheeked innocence even though she is wearing nothing under her transparent plastic mac.

It is the faces one returns to; the various ways in which people negotiate the uncertain contract between themselves and the stranger with the camera, sometimes becoming demure, sometimes uncomfortable, sometimes returning its gaze intently or casually. Some of the most powerful portraits here are the hardest to read. Sharon, a young black woman photographed on the street in Brixton, has a presence that is both self-contained and defiant, her engagement with the camera so uncompromising that she seems to be daring it to contain her.

Encountering some of these portraits in an earlier iteration of this book, the enigma that is Derek Ridgers deepened for me. When I first crossed paths with him in the mid-1980s, he was working as a music photographer for *NME*, where I also worked as a journalist. Back then, he came across as a guarded, slightly aloof individual, singularly uninterested in the passionate factionalism that fuelled the paper's music journalism at the time. It was not until several years later that I became aware of his other more personal body of work, including some of the portraits gathered here.

Unlike his music photography, where the subjects are famous to one degree or another, these portraits are determinedly democratic: a visual record of the myriad young people who, for a time, defined themselves by their adherence to a tribe or a style, sometimes becoming well-known faces within a subcultural milieu. One cannot but wonder where they are now and how their lives have unfolded since those heady days of youthful and flamboyant self-reinvention.

As time passes, this kind of observational photography attains a new importance, becoming a kind of visual anthropology of a bygone era. In this context, Ridgers' adherence to the governing idea of democratic detachment – the observer, 'constantly on the margins with a camera' – seems even more astute, even if, as he insists, it was utterly instinctive. Interestingly, he happened on photography by accident, when the advertising agency he worked for in the 1970s gave him a new Miranda camera to try out, having landed a campaign for the parent company, Minolta. This lack of formal training, coupled with that utterly unaffected air of aloofness I sensed in him all those years ago, has somehow worked in his favour as a photographer.

'When I go to a club, I am stand-offish', he says, 'because I'm concentrating on stuff – who to photograph, how and where to photograph them. It's very serious. It took me a while to pluck up the courage to approach people, but I realised that all they need to know is that you are sincere.'That, too, is evident in the images gathered here. As ever, they tell us as much about the person behind the camera as the person in front of it. In these portraits, nothing is imposed; Ridgers simply allows his subjects to be themselves in the defining moment when he presses the shutter.

This book is a document of a time and a place that now seems impossibly distant, even as its traces linger among today's more knowing, endlessly referential, globally interconnected pop landscape. Time passes, styles change, ordinary people, once young and fearless, fade into the maw of history. Photographs remain; a complex kind of evidence, brimming with clues, details and signifiers; in this instance, they evoke a particularly creative period in the history of British youth culture, which, in all its tribal differences, was essentially about belonging and identity. It took someone who felt he did not belong to stand back and observe that extended moment in all its strange and sometimes startling diversity of self-expression.

Sean O'Hagan, January 2024.

Names unknown, Portobello Road 1979.

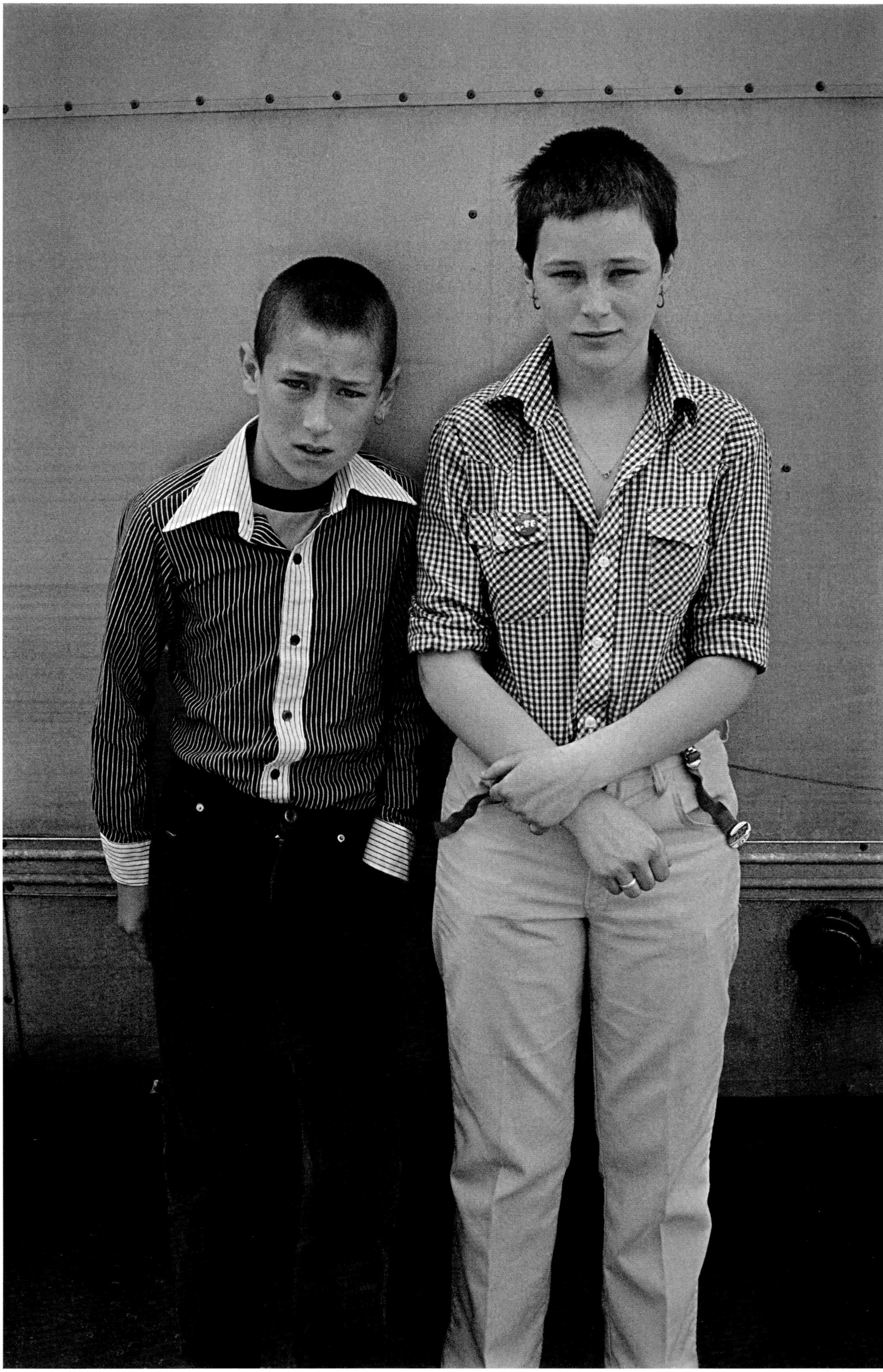

Jenny, Alice In Wonderland 1984.

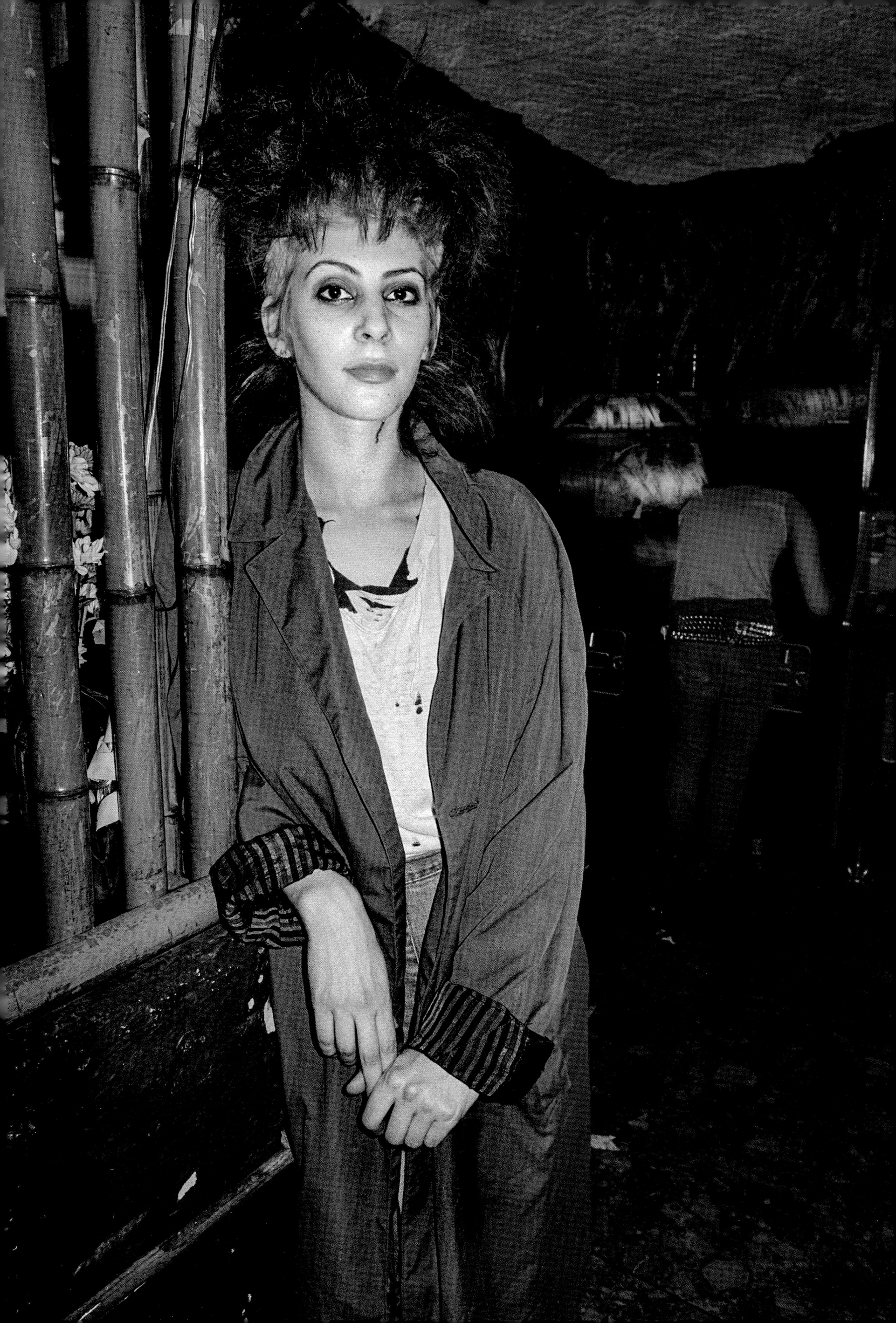

Kate, Bowie Night at Billy's, Soho 1978.

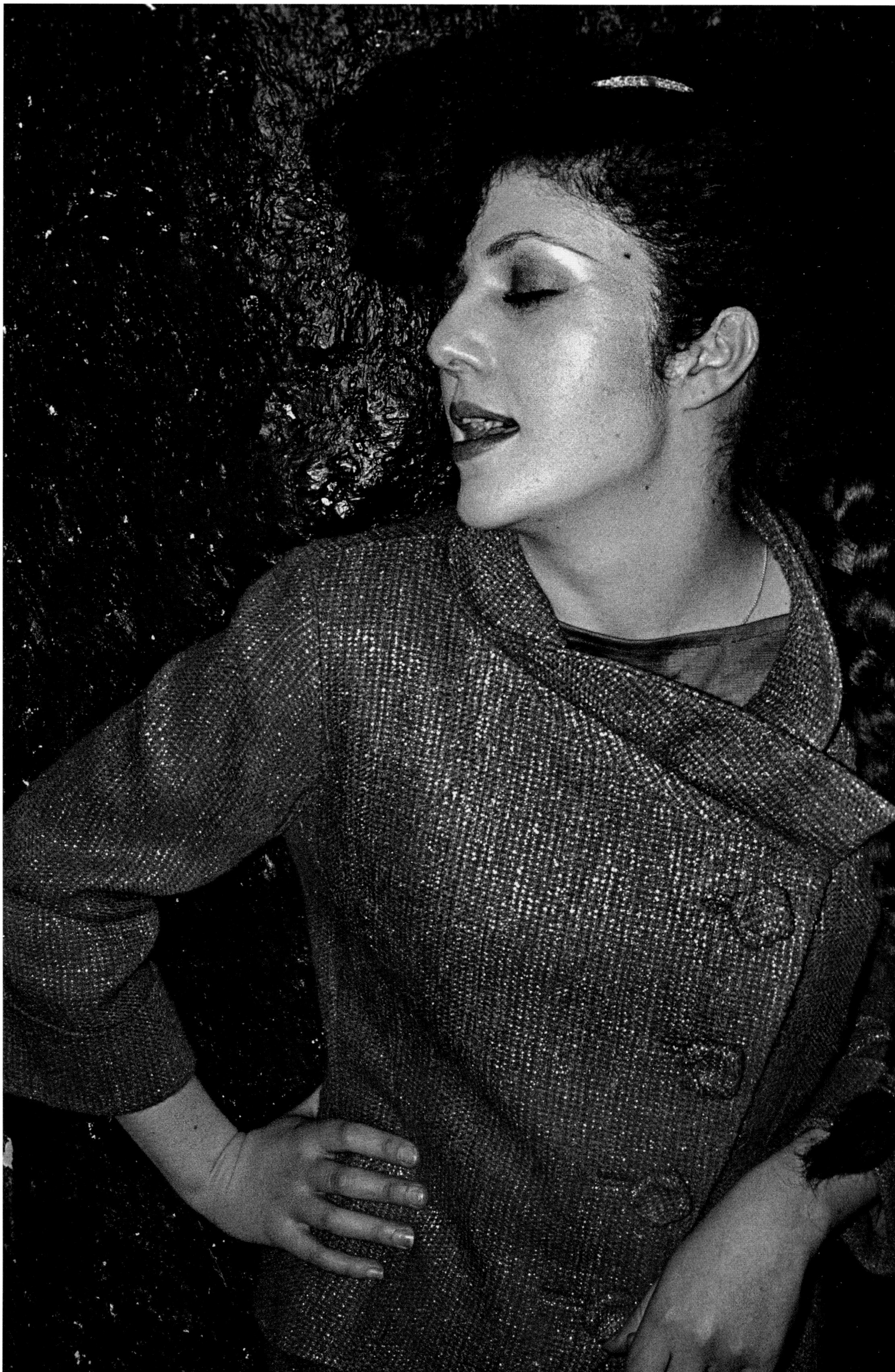

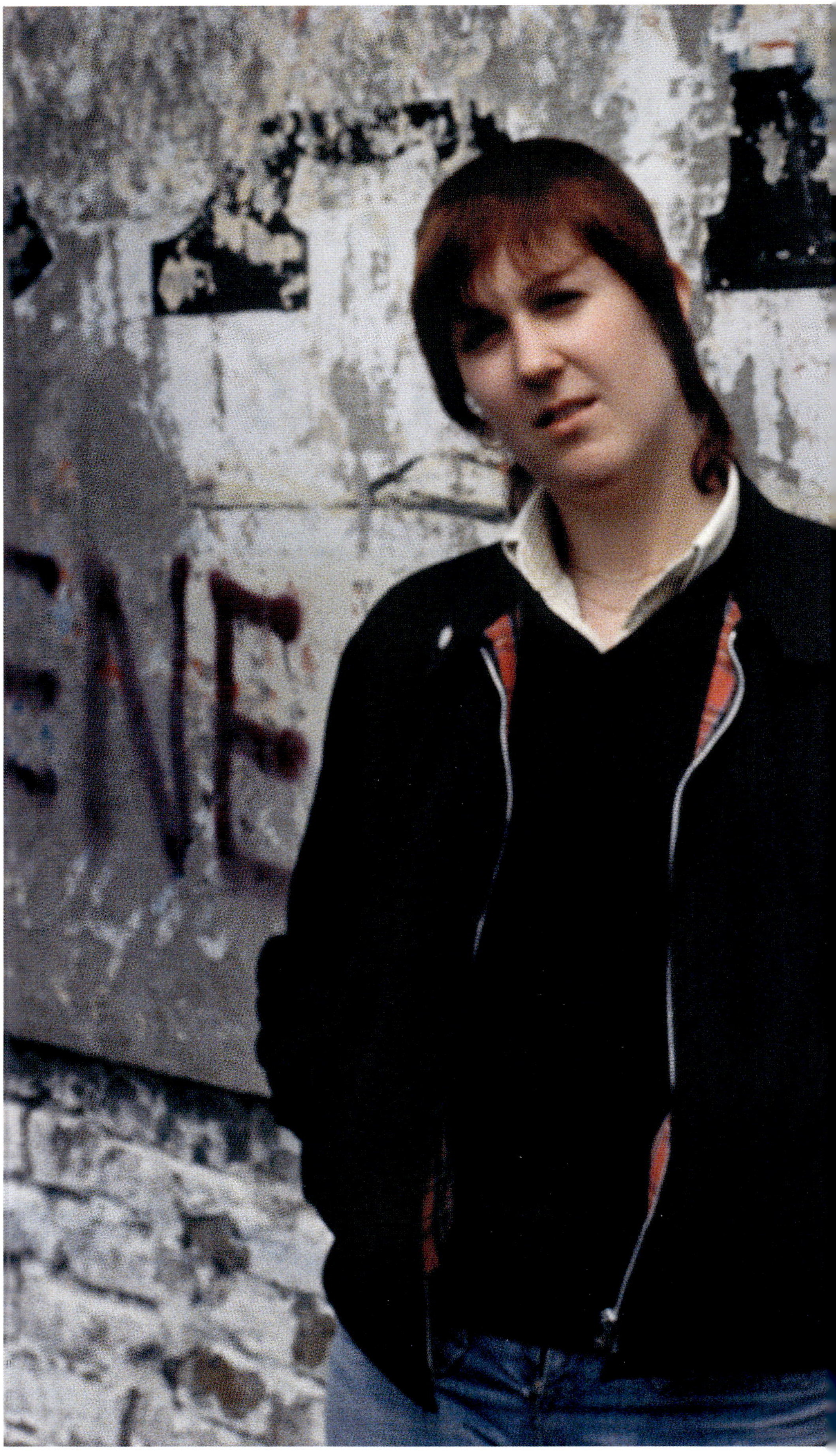

Kate & Lesley,
Shoreditch 1979.

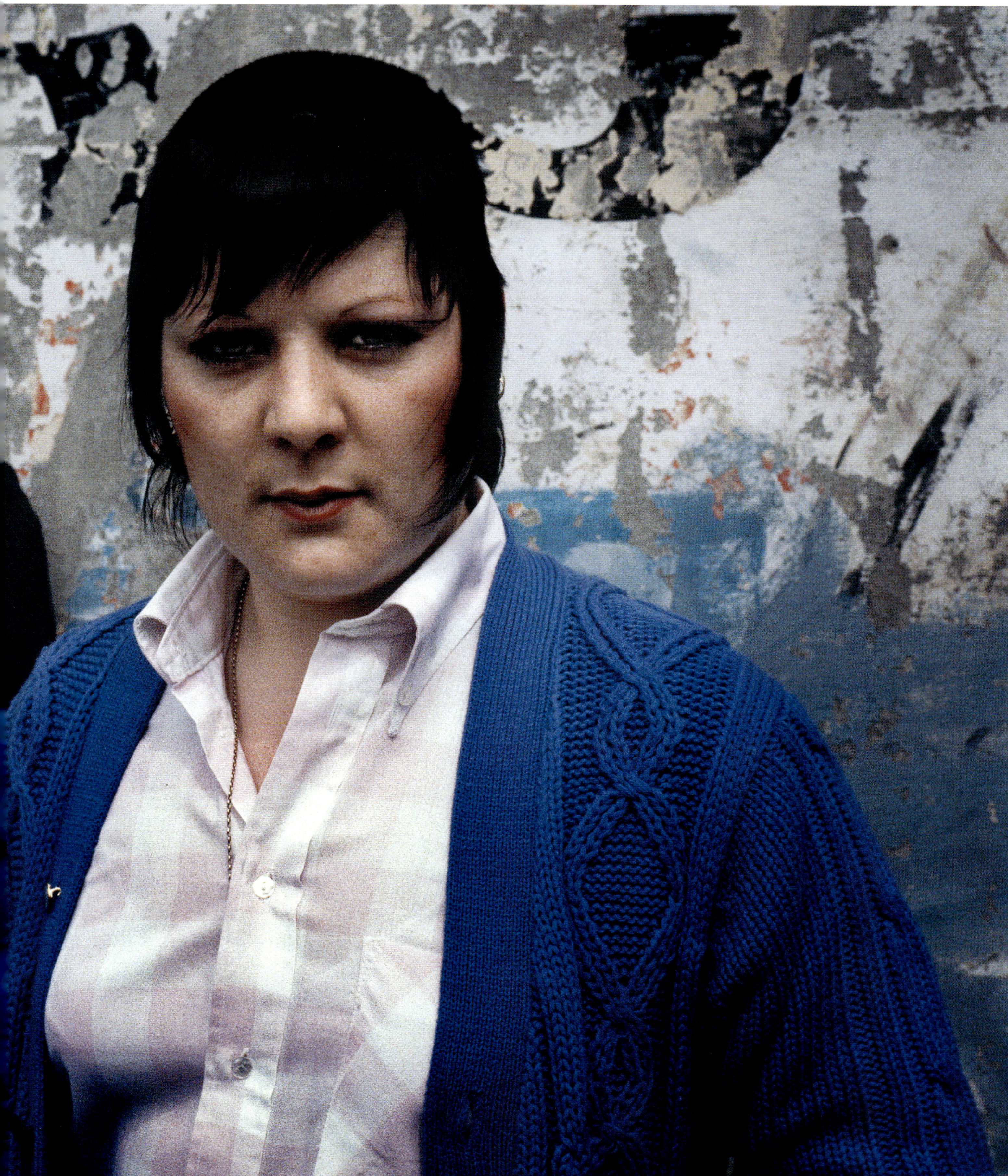

Alex, Hounslow 1980.

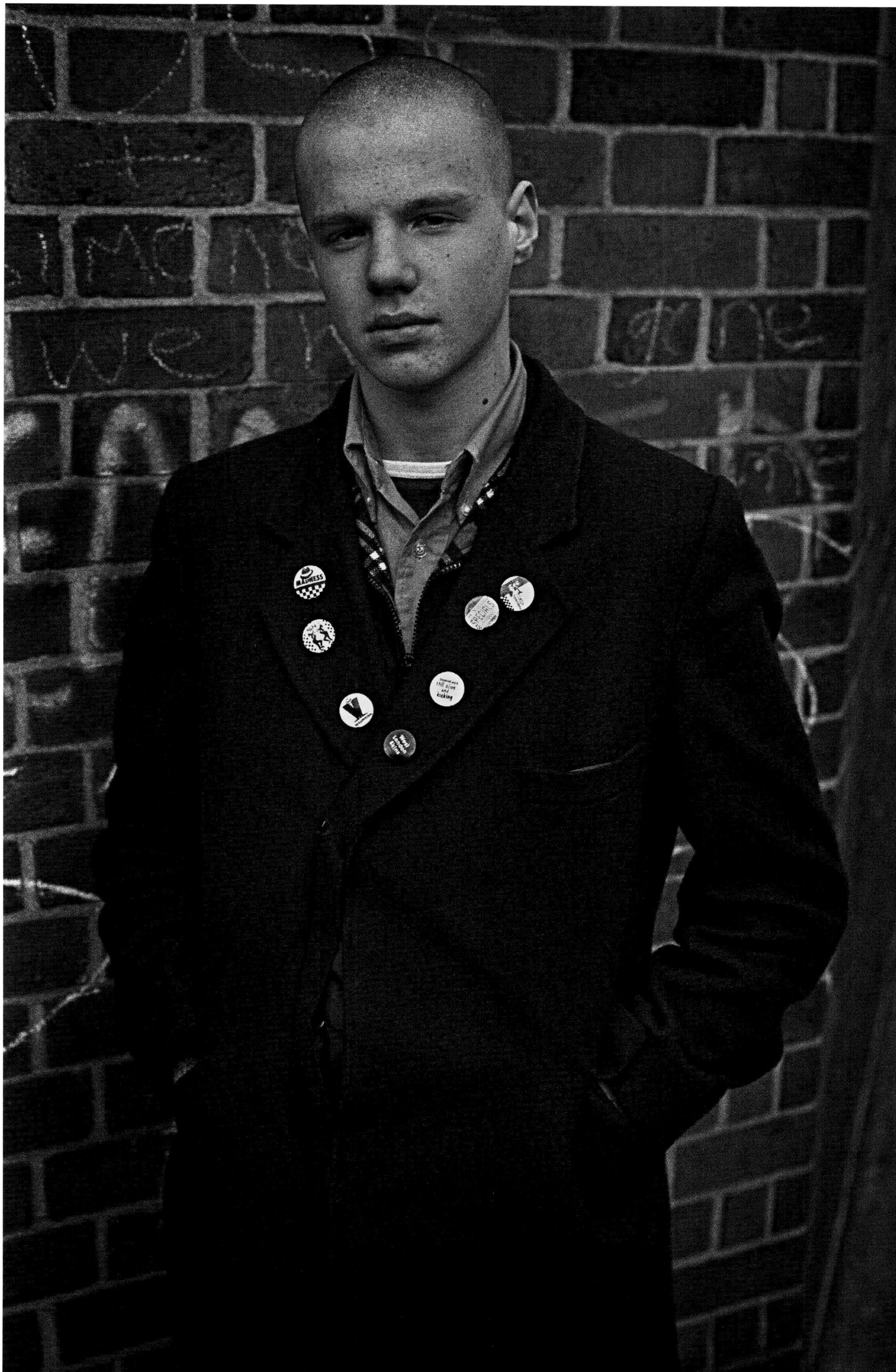
MADNESS

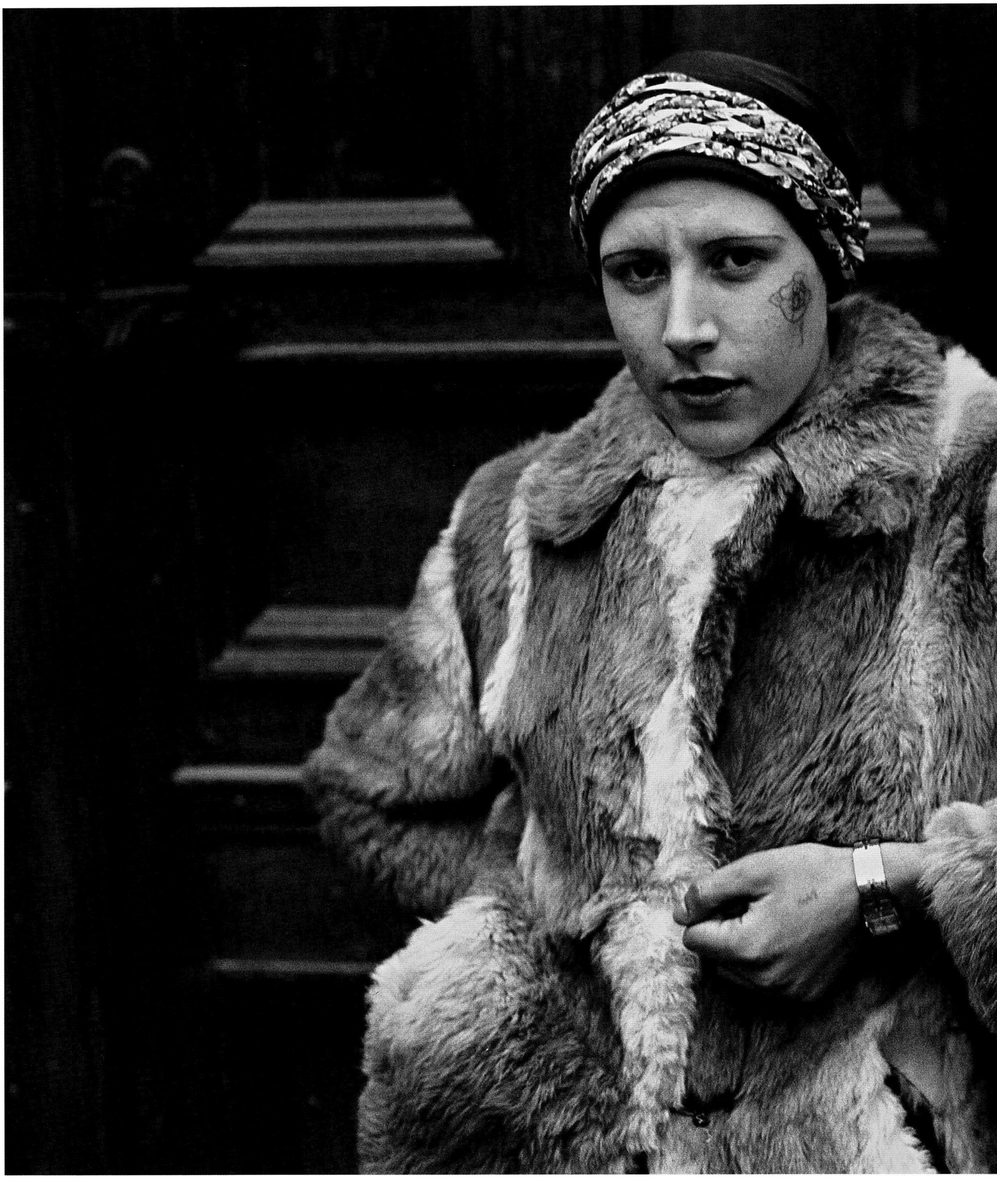

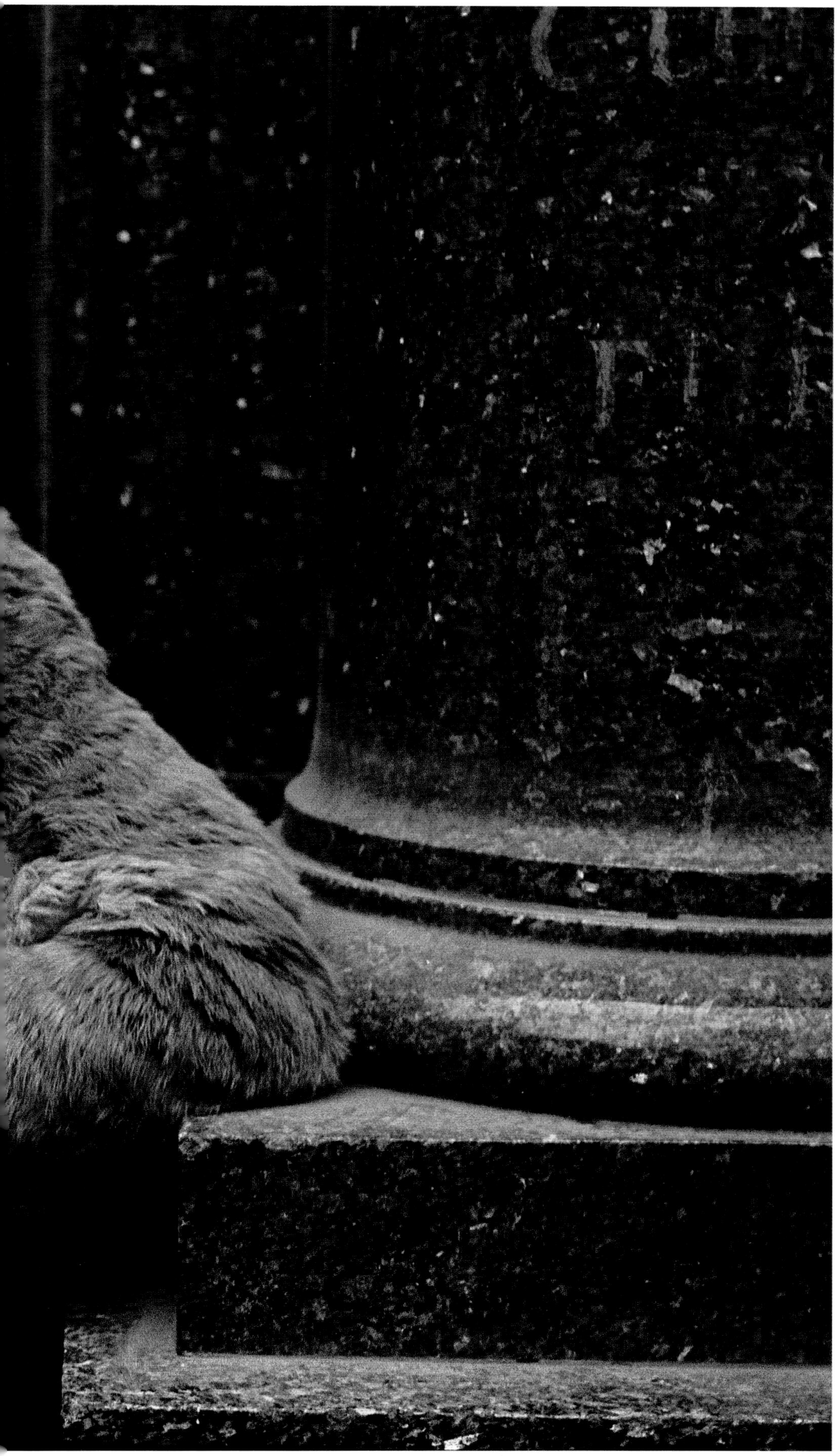

Lyn, Piccadilly 1980.

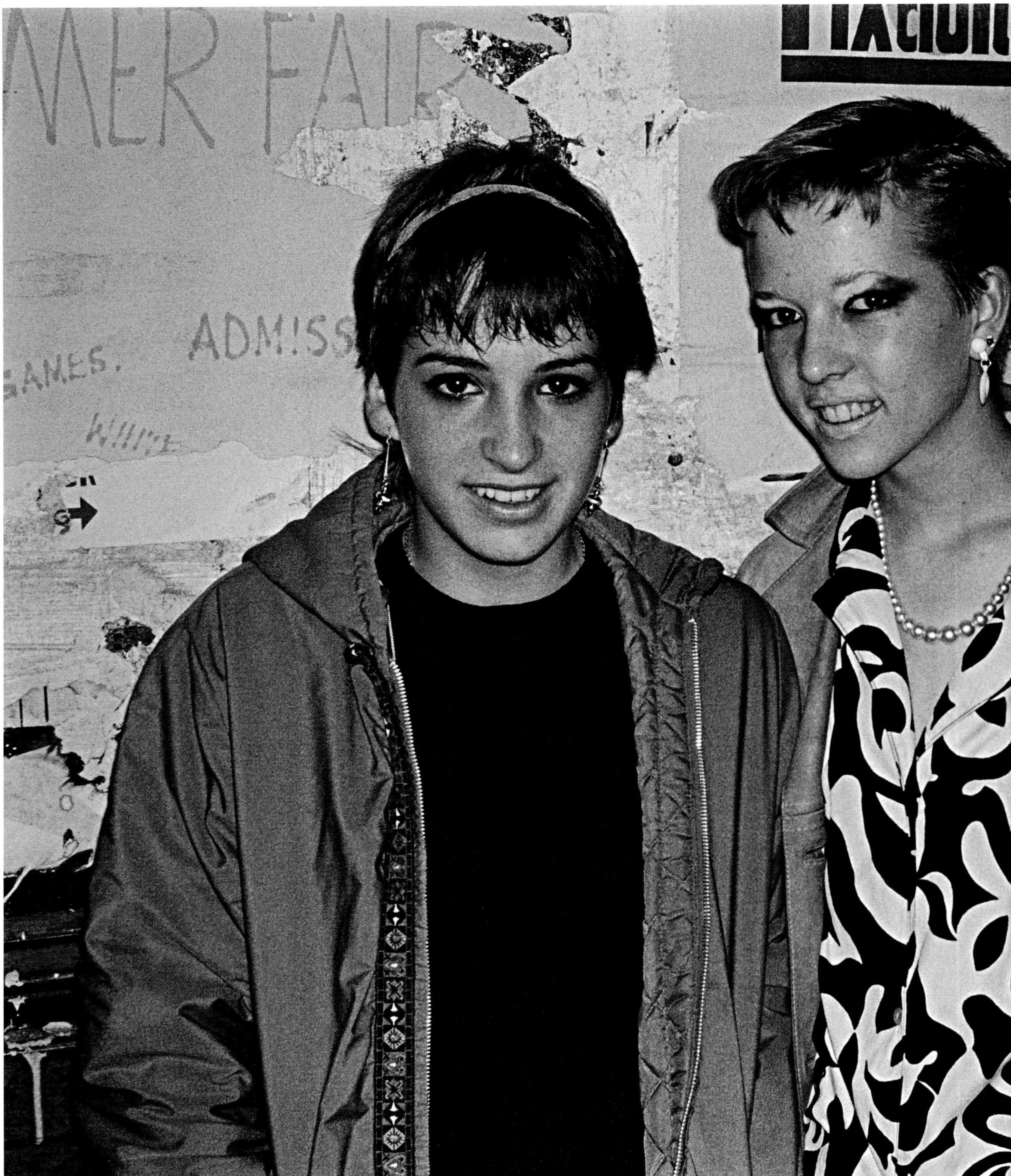
MER FAIR
ADM!SS
GAMES.

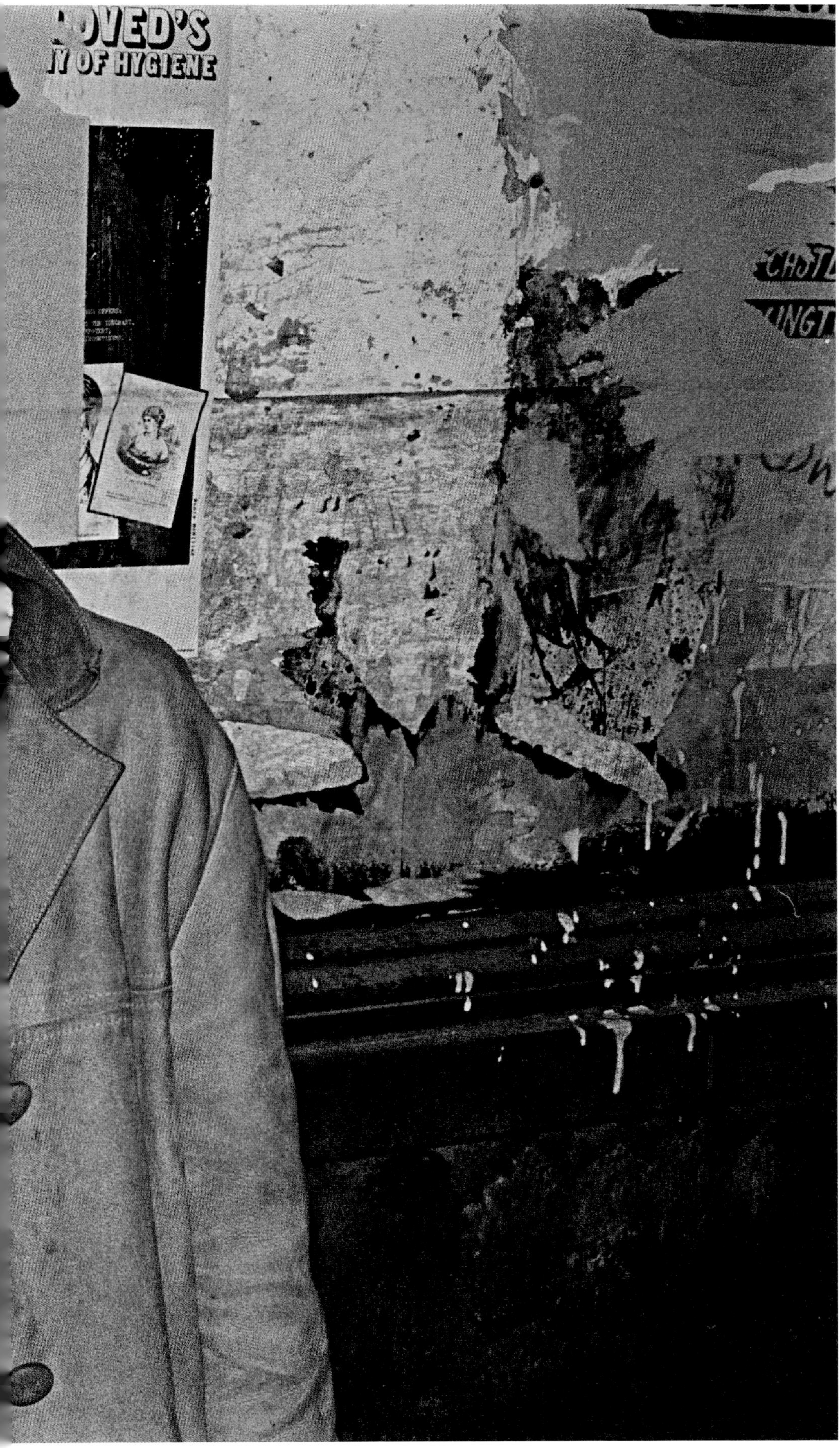

Kate & Jane, outside The Wellington pub, Waterloo 1979.

Judy aka Tank, North Kensington 1981.

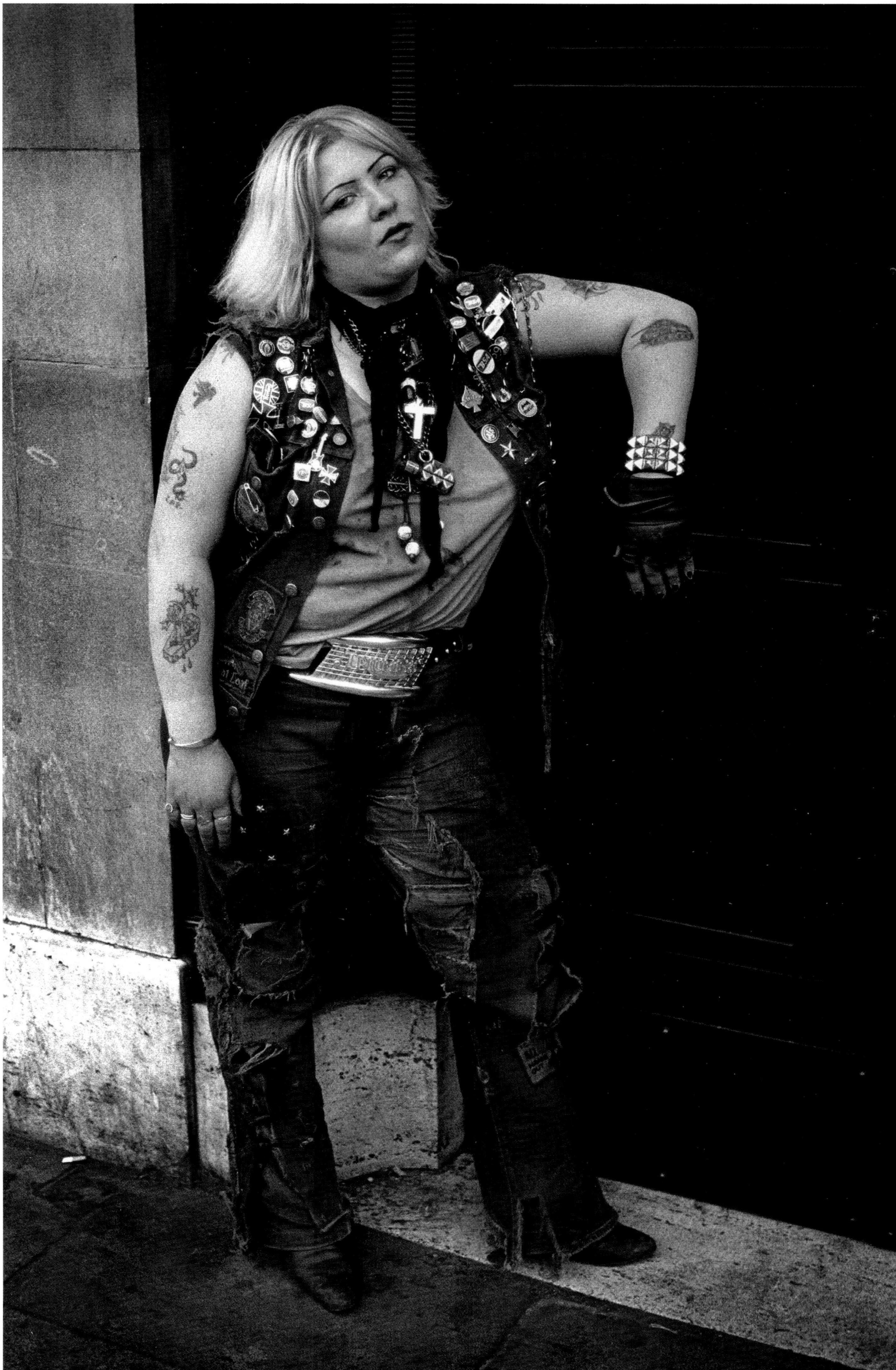

Debbie & Caroline, Brighton 1980.

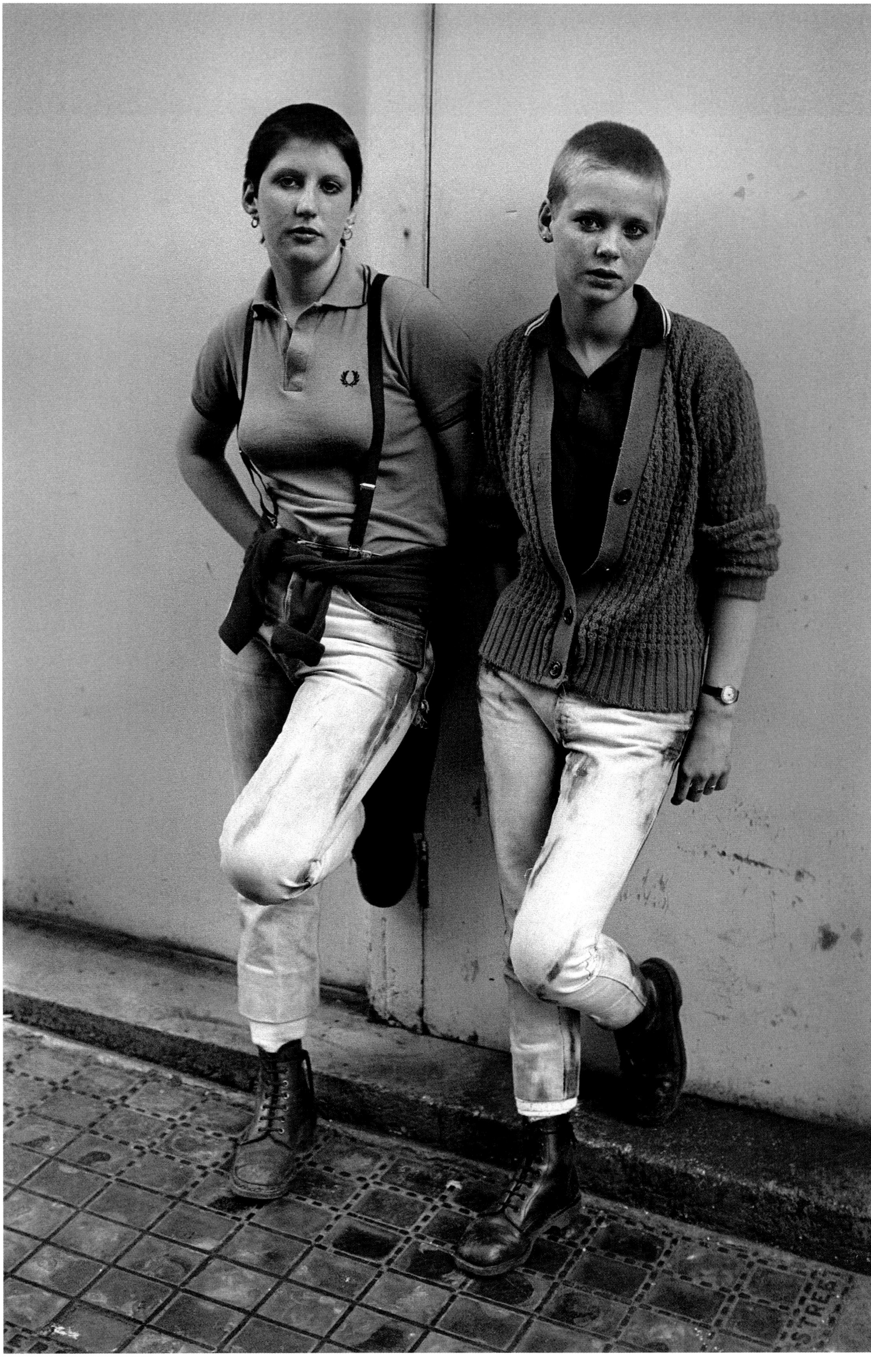

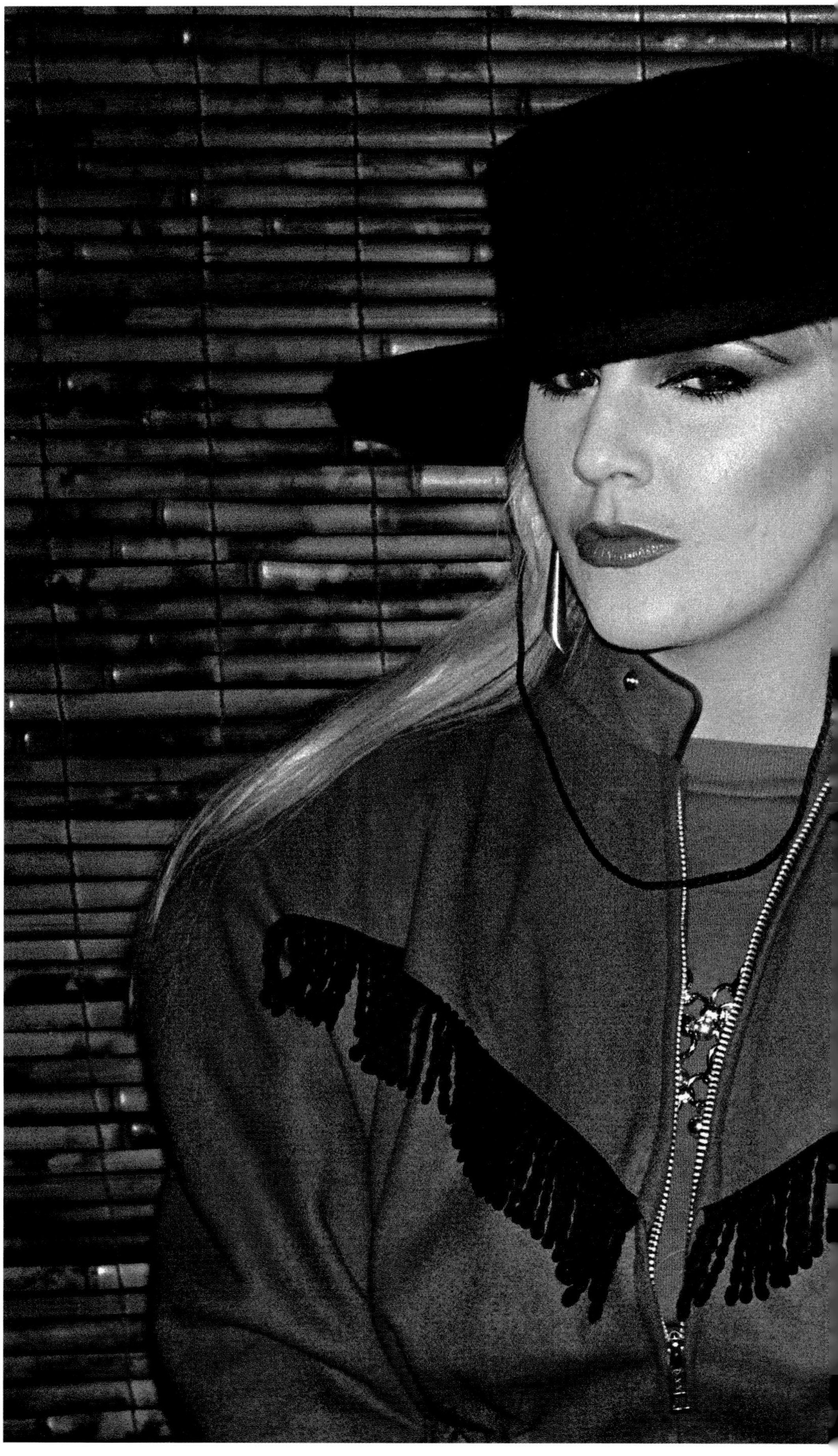

Karen & Marilyn, Blitz, Covent Garden 1979.

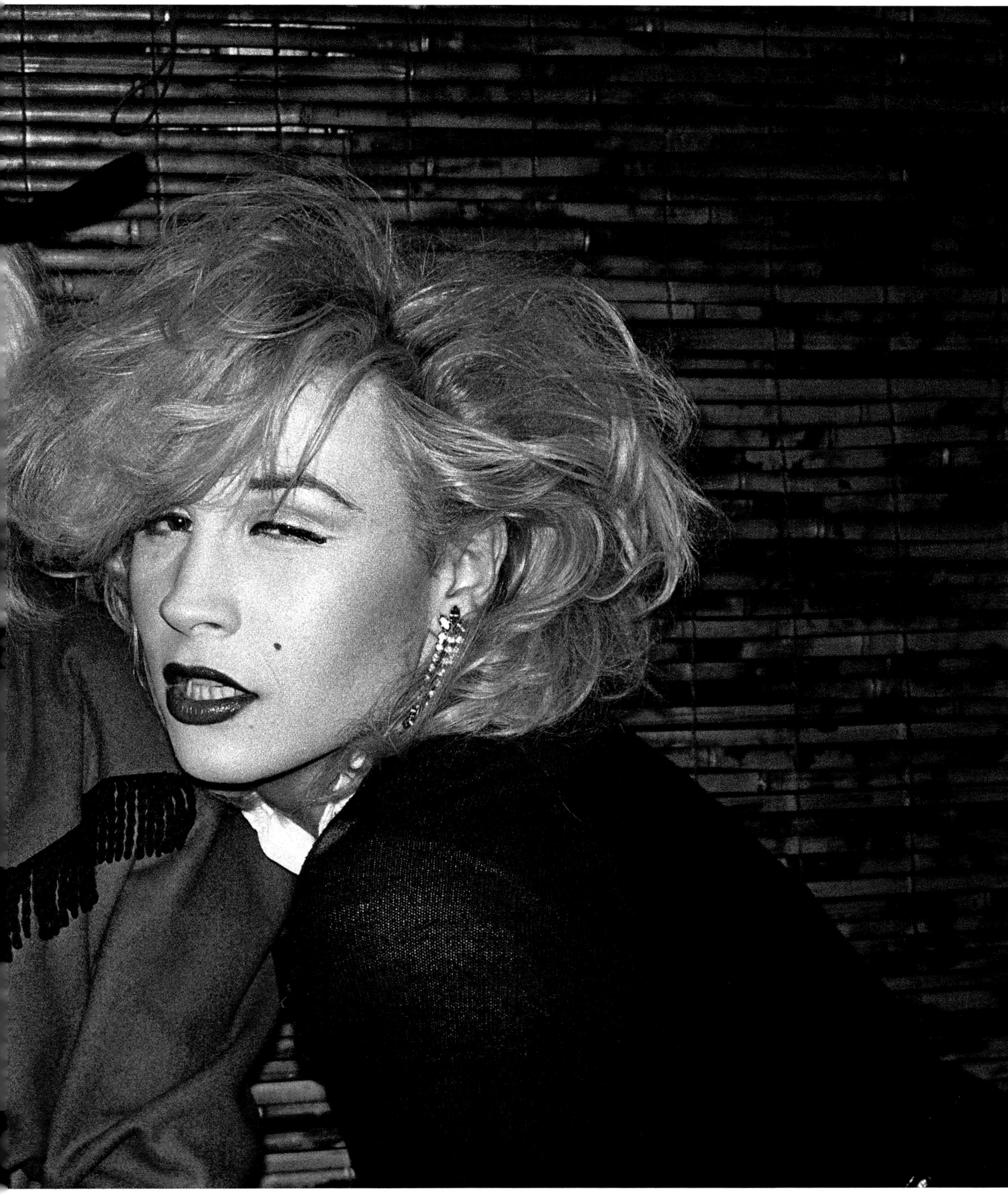

Tuinol Barry, King's Road, Chelsea 1983.

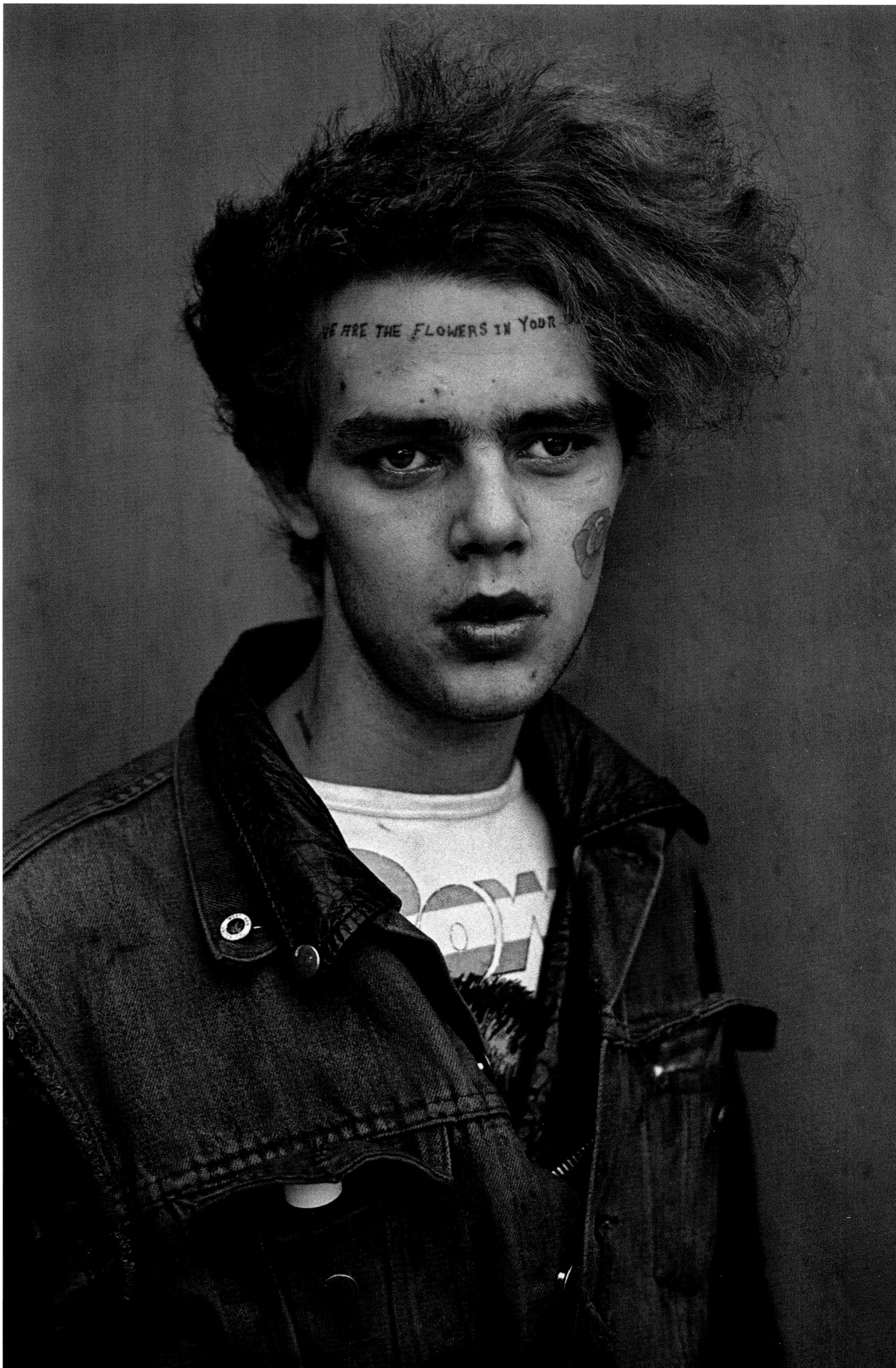
ARE THE FLOWERS IN YOUR

Name unknown, Chelsea 1983.

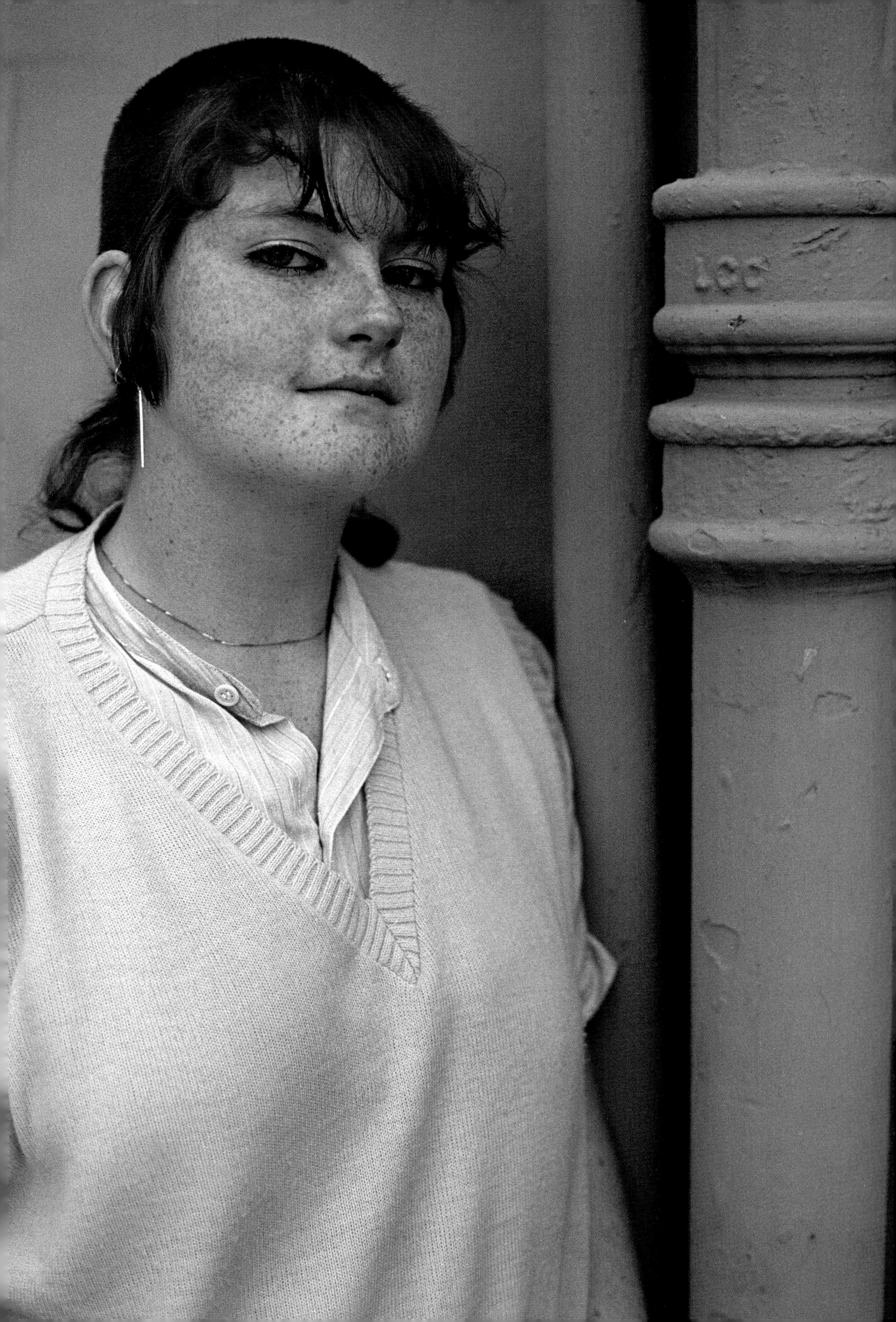

Names unknown,
Shoreditch 1979.

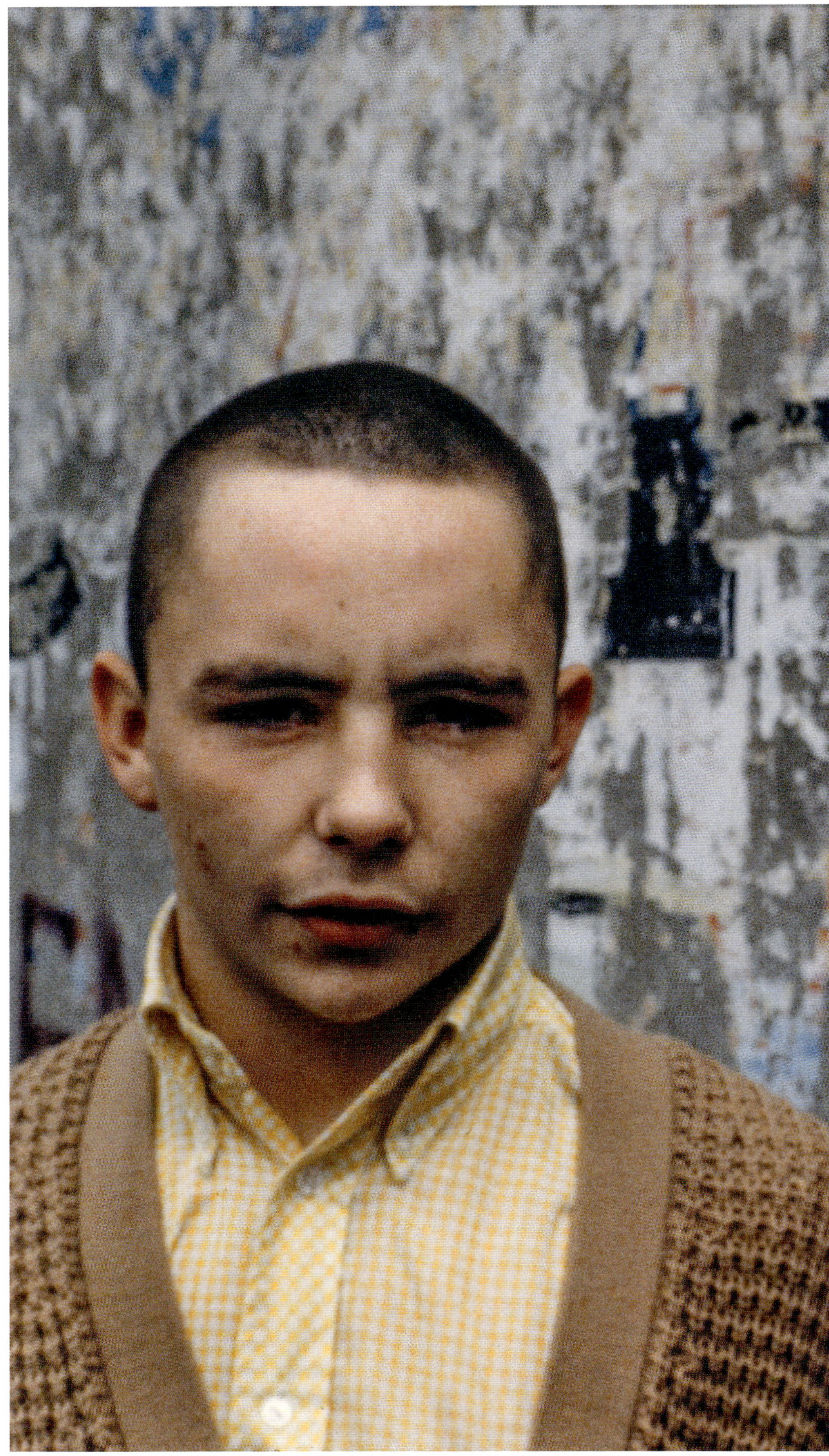

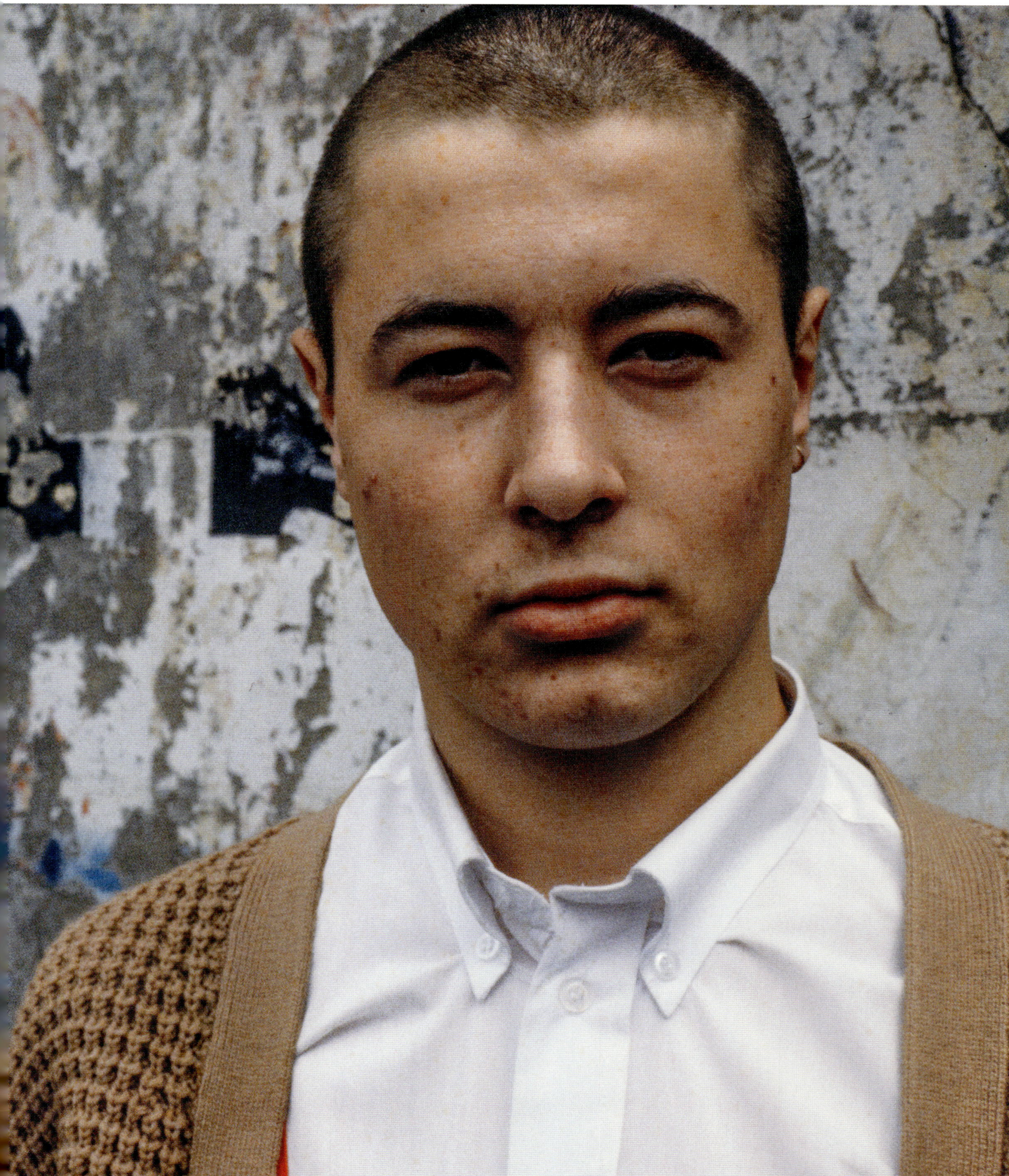

Tosh, Leicester Square 1983.

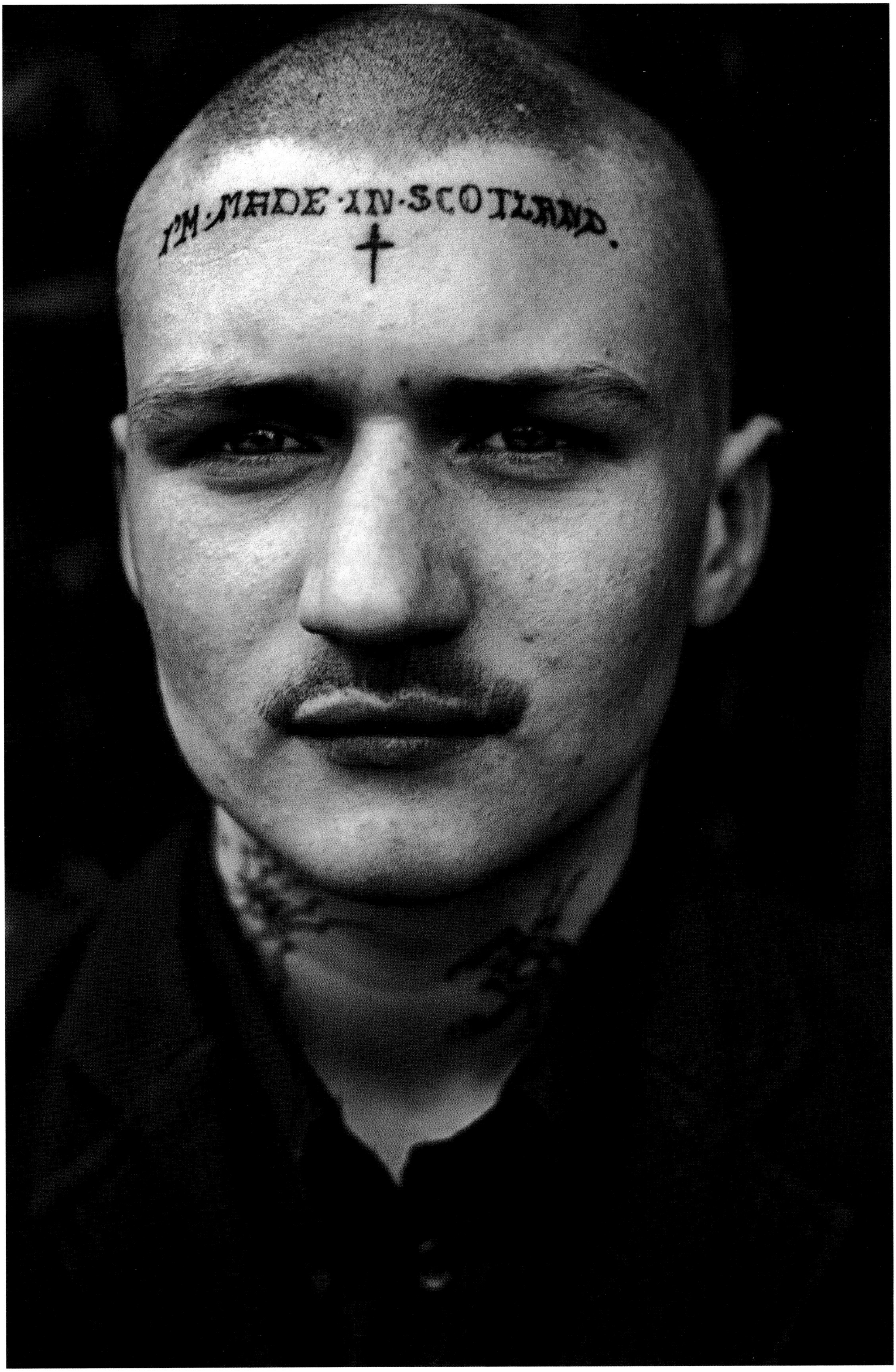
I'M·MADE·IN·SCOTLAND.

Dawnie, Skin Two, Soho 1983.

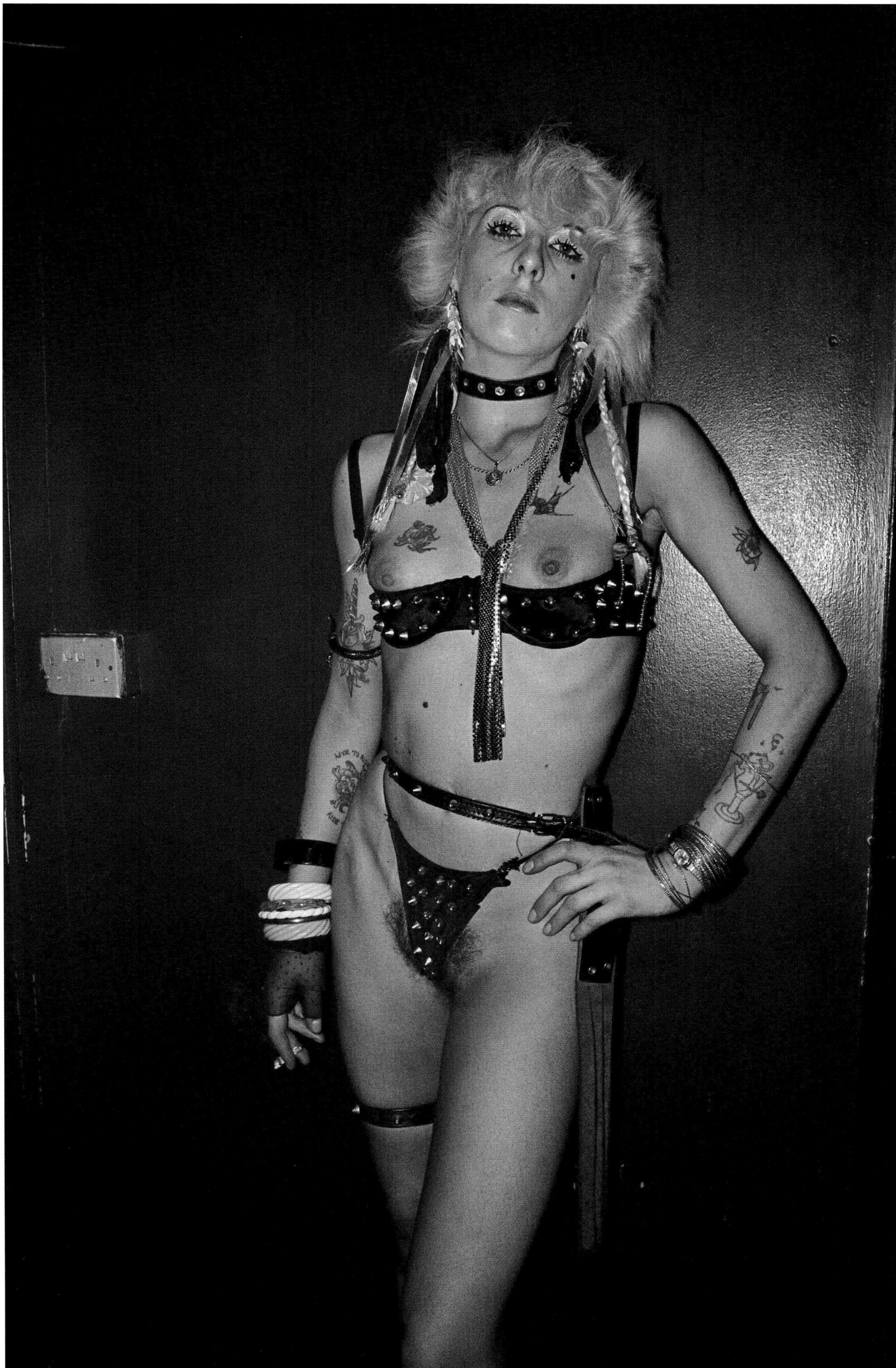

Theresa, Hell,
Covent Garden 1980.

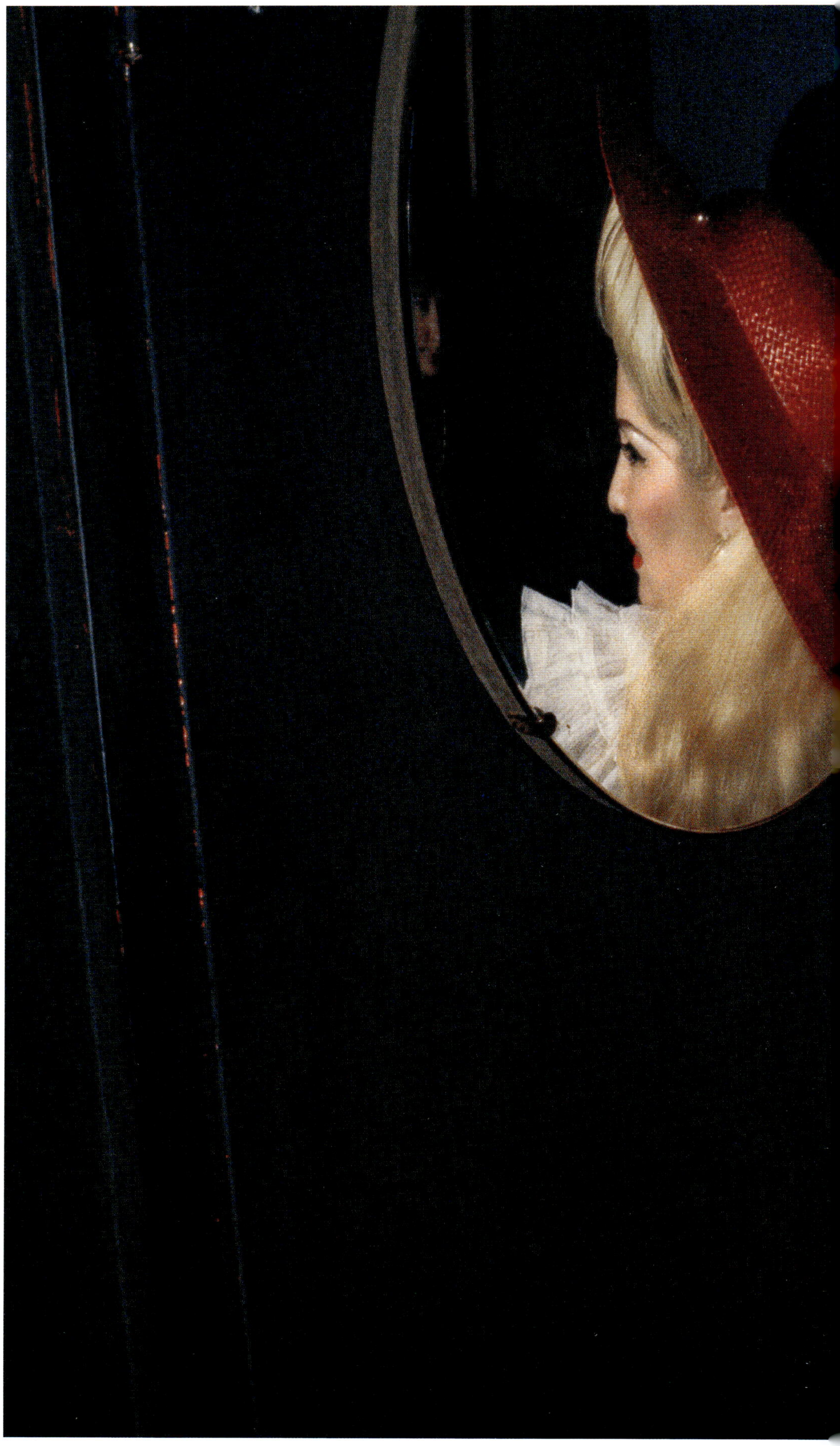

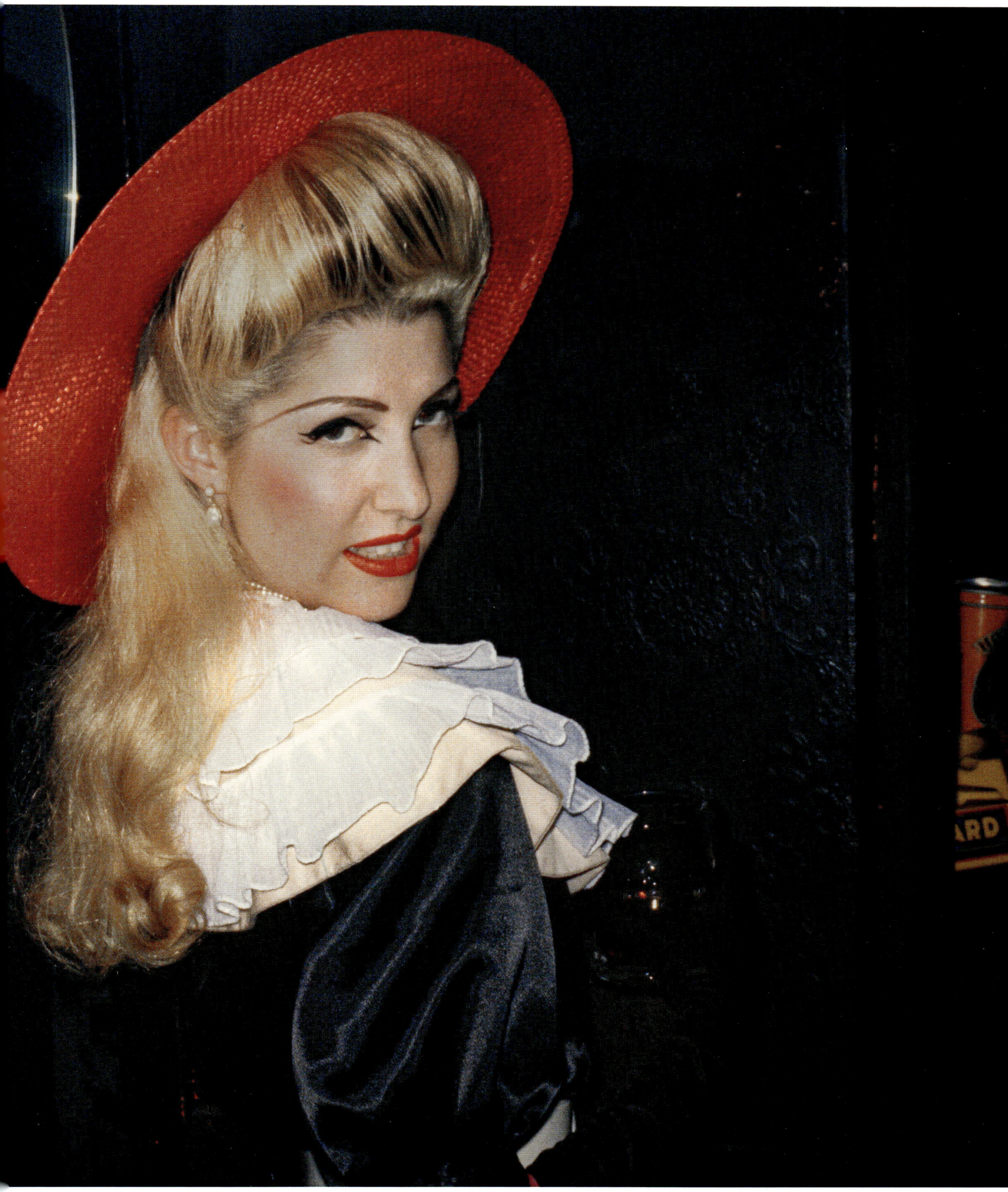

Iggy aka Belsen, Soho 1983.

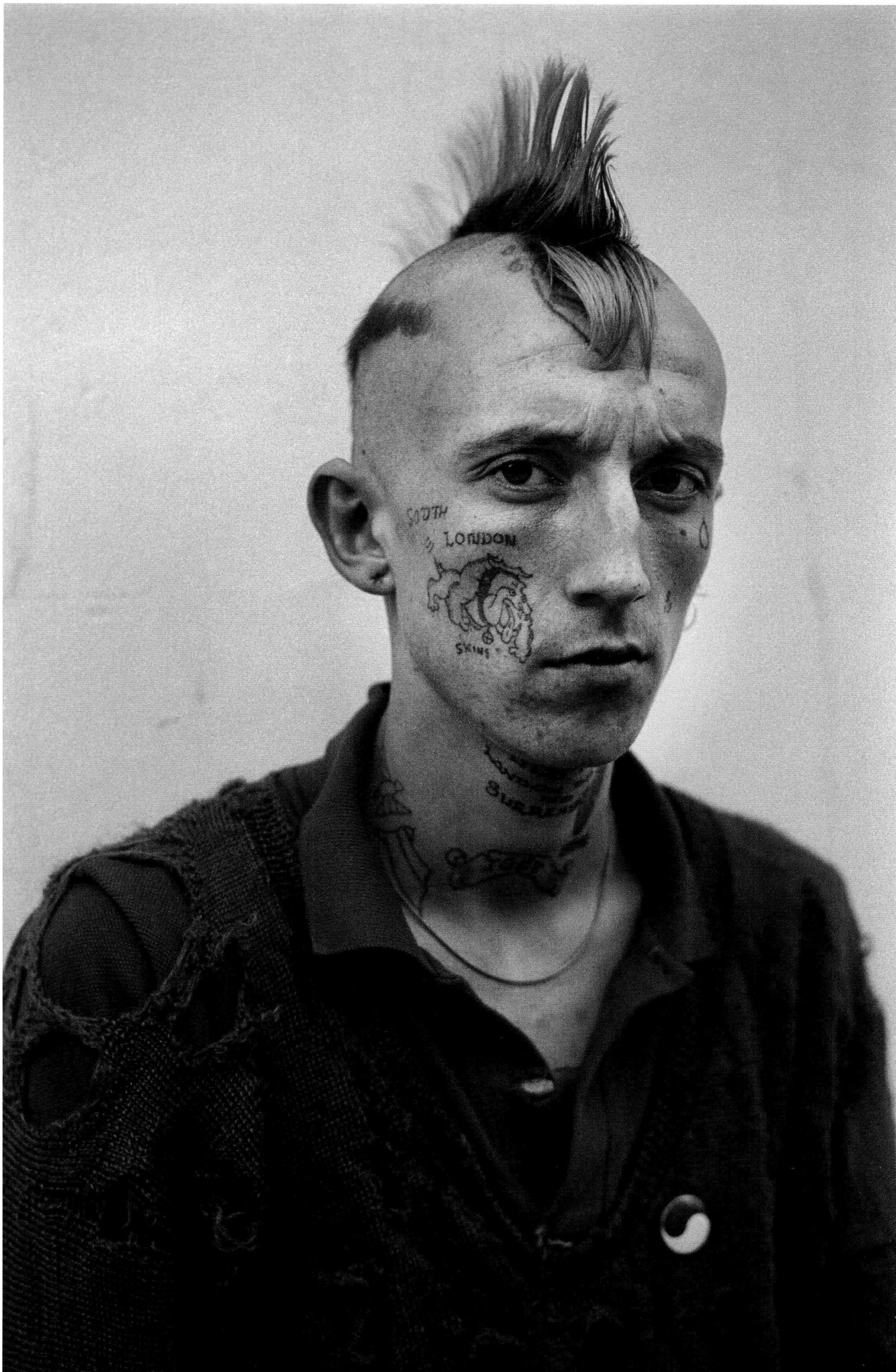
SOUTH
LONDON
SKINS

Paul, Camden Palace 1982.

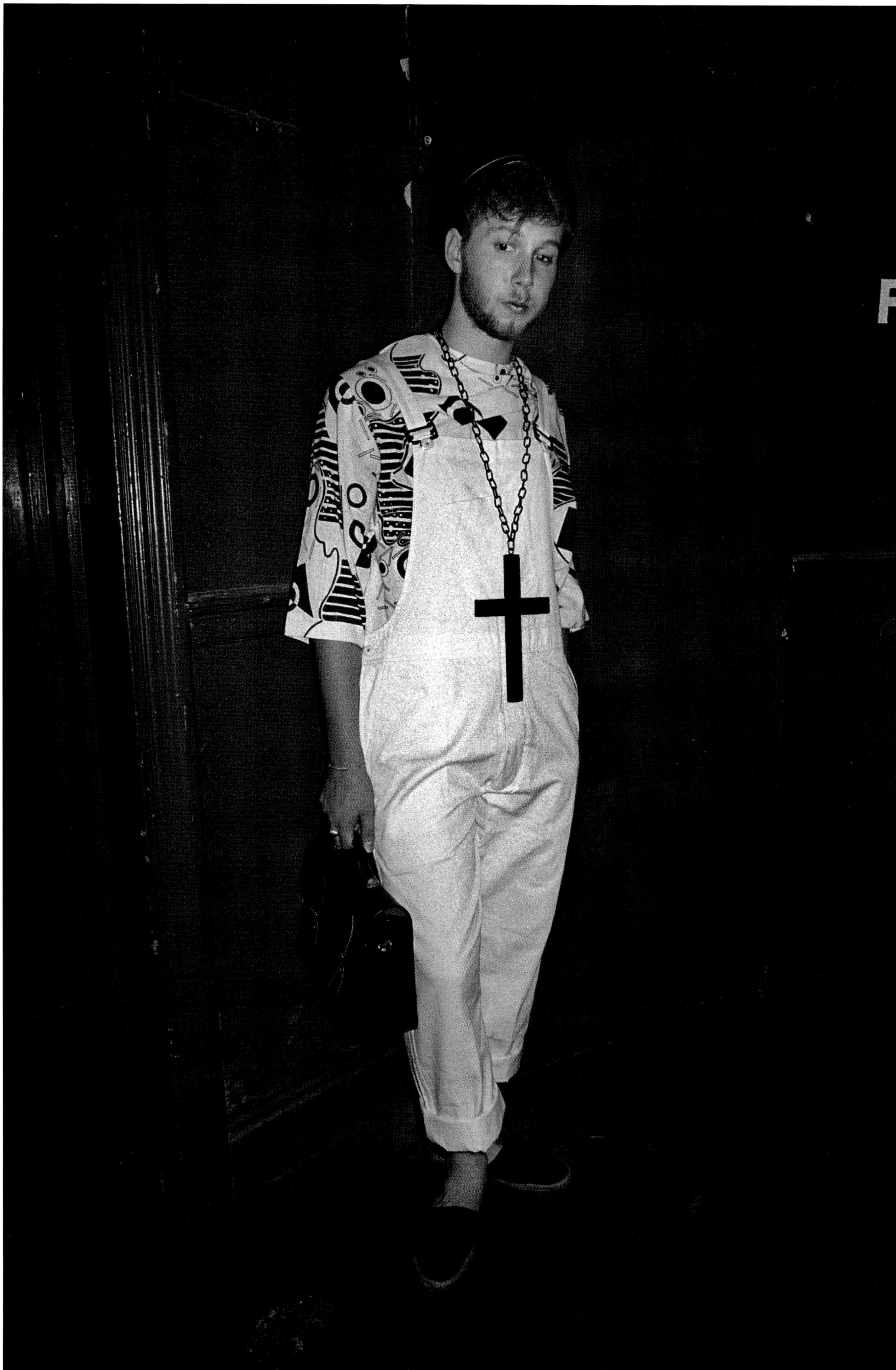

Letty, King's Road, Chelsea 1984.

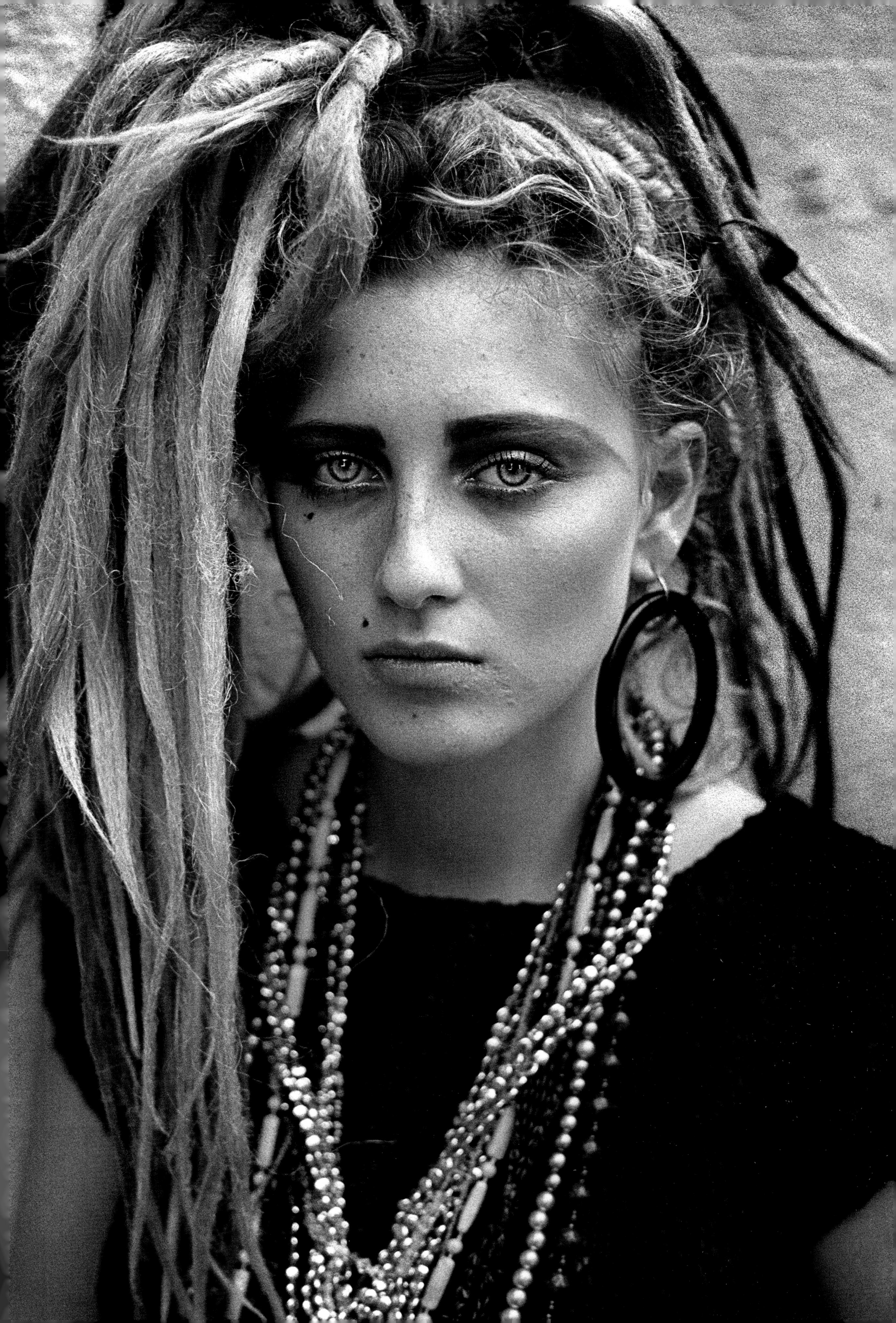

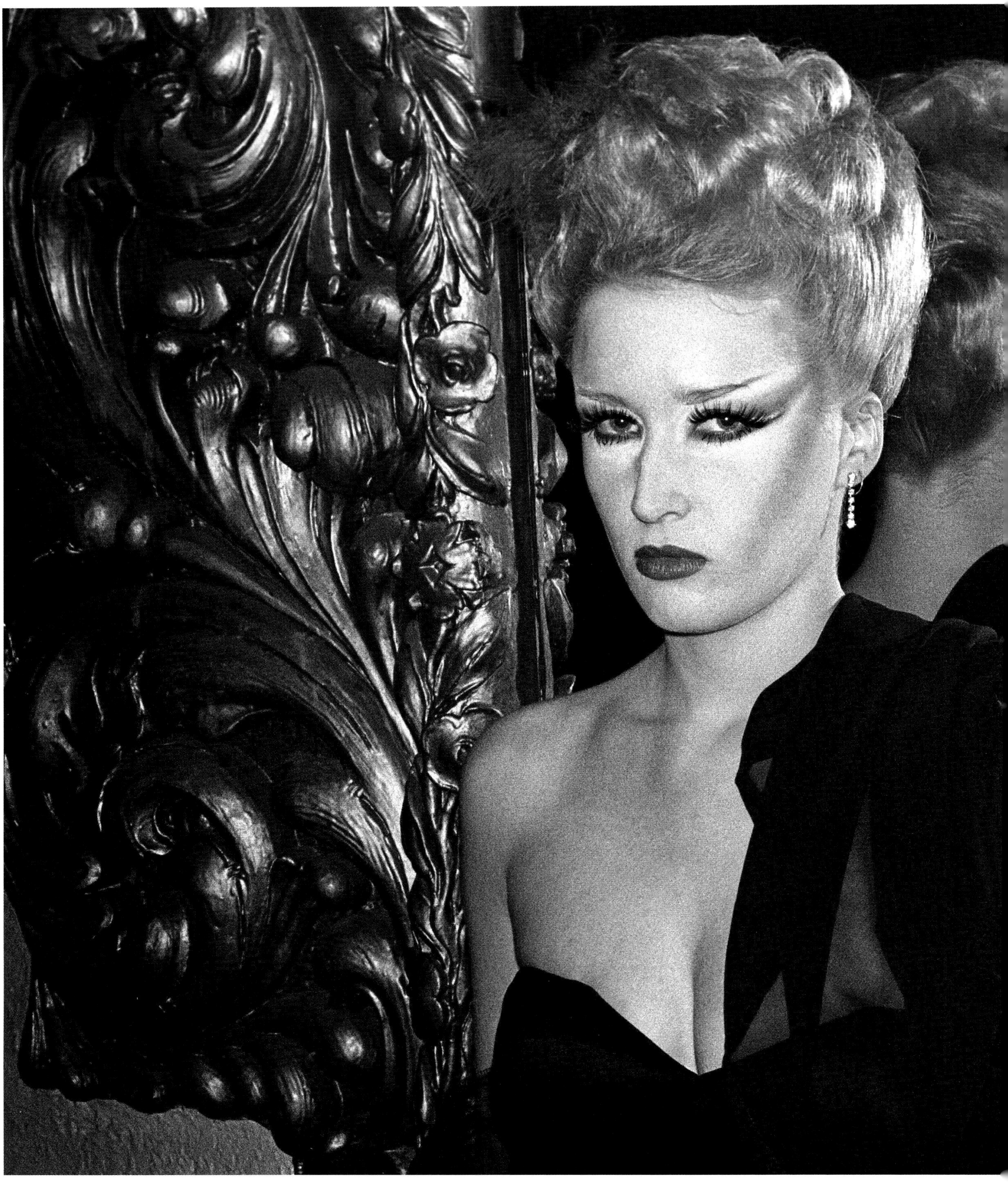

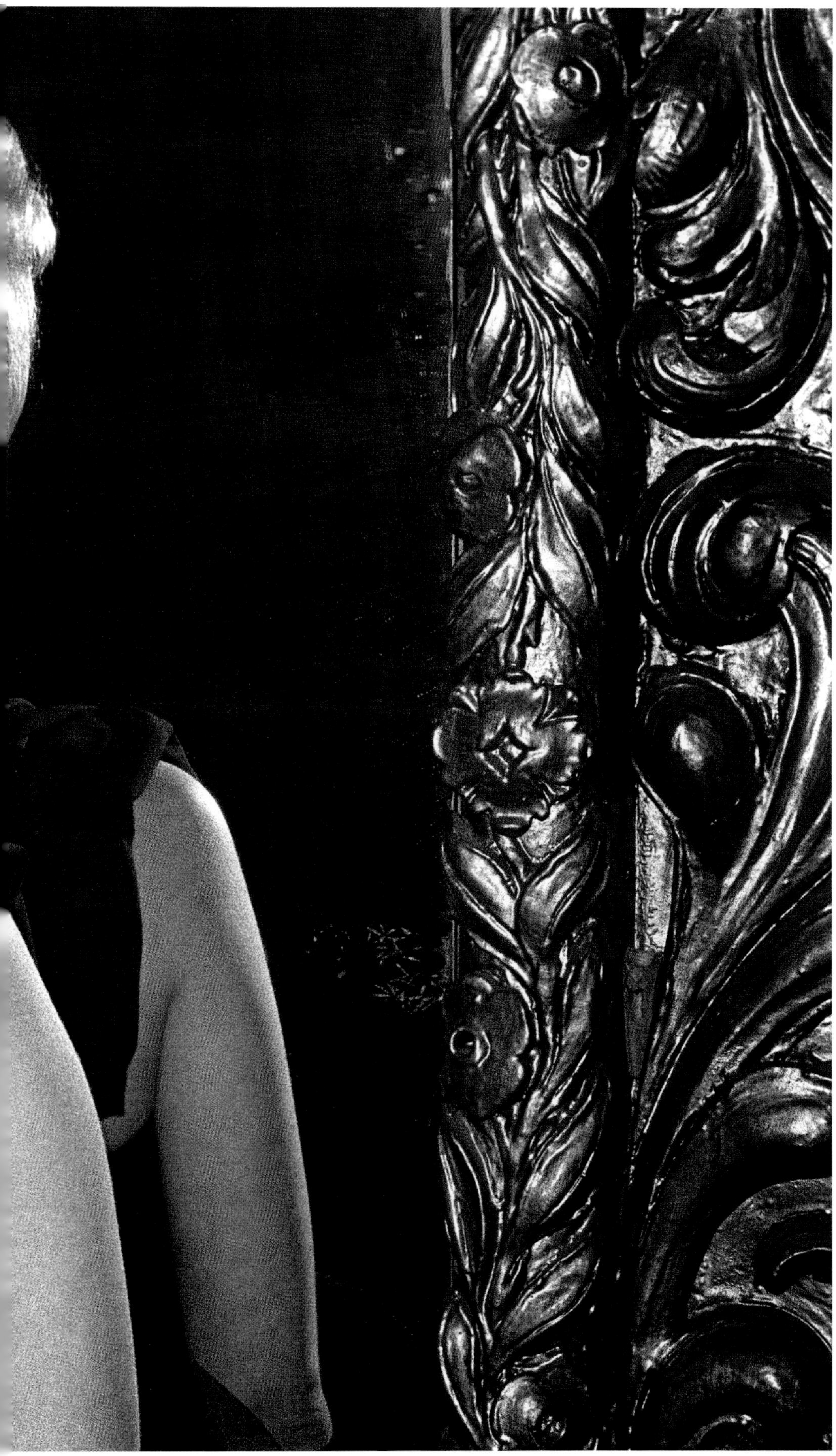

Paula, People's Palace,
Finsbury Park 1981.

Yasmine, King's Road, Chelsea 1984.

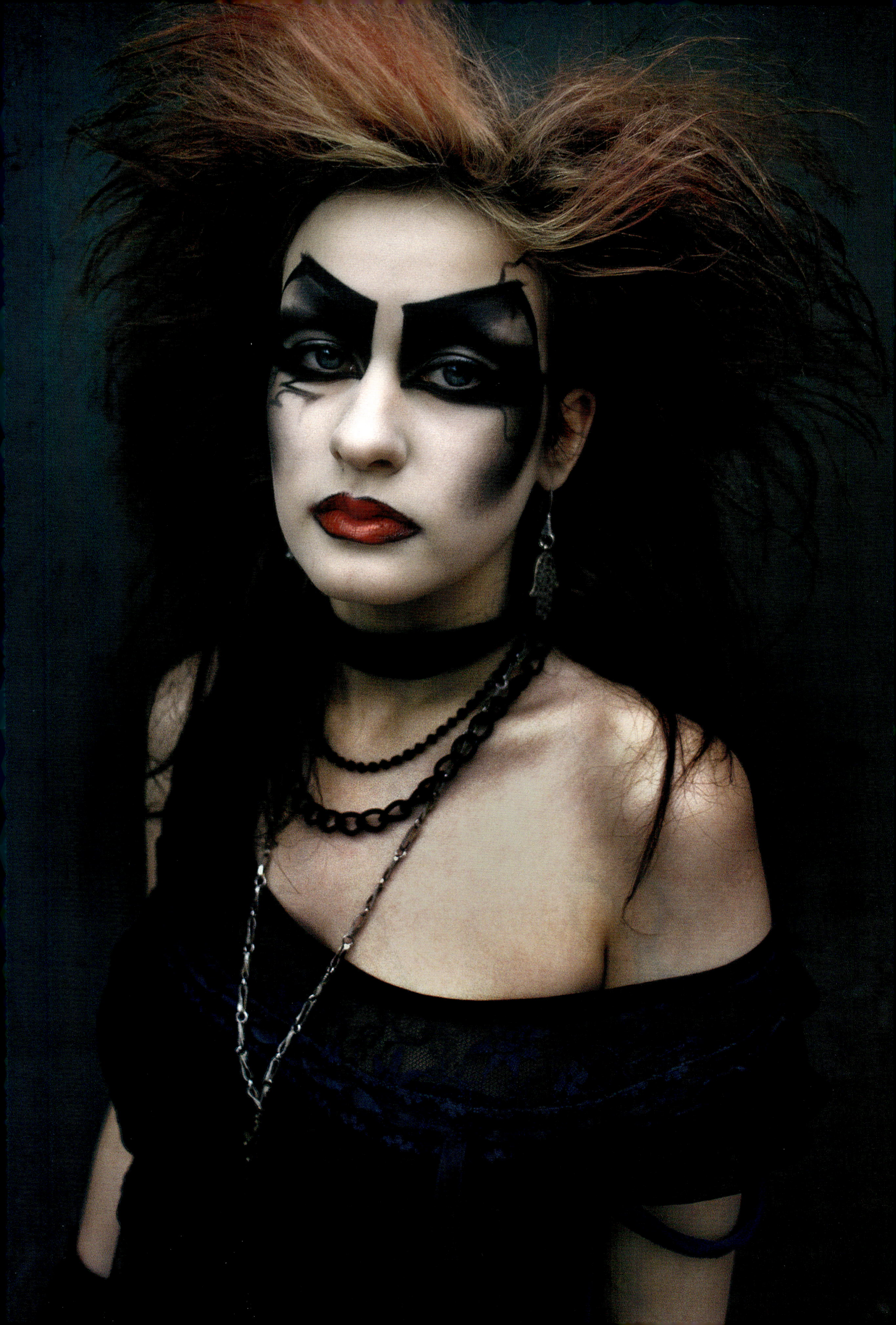

Susie, Chelsea 1982.

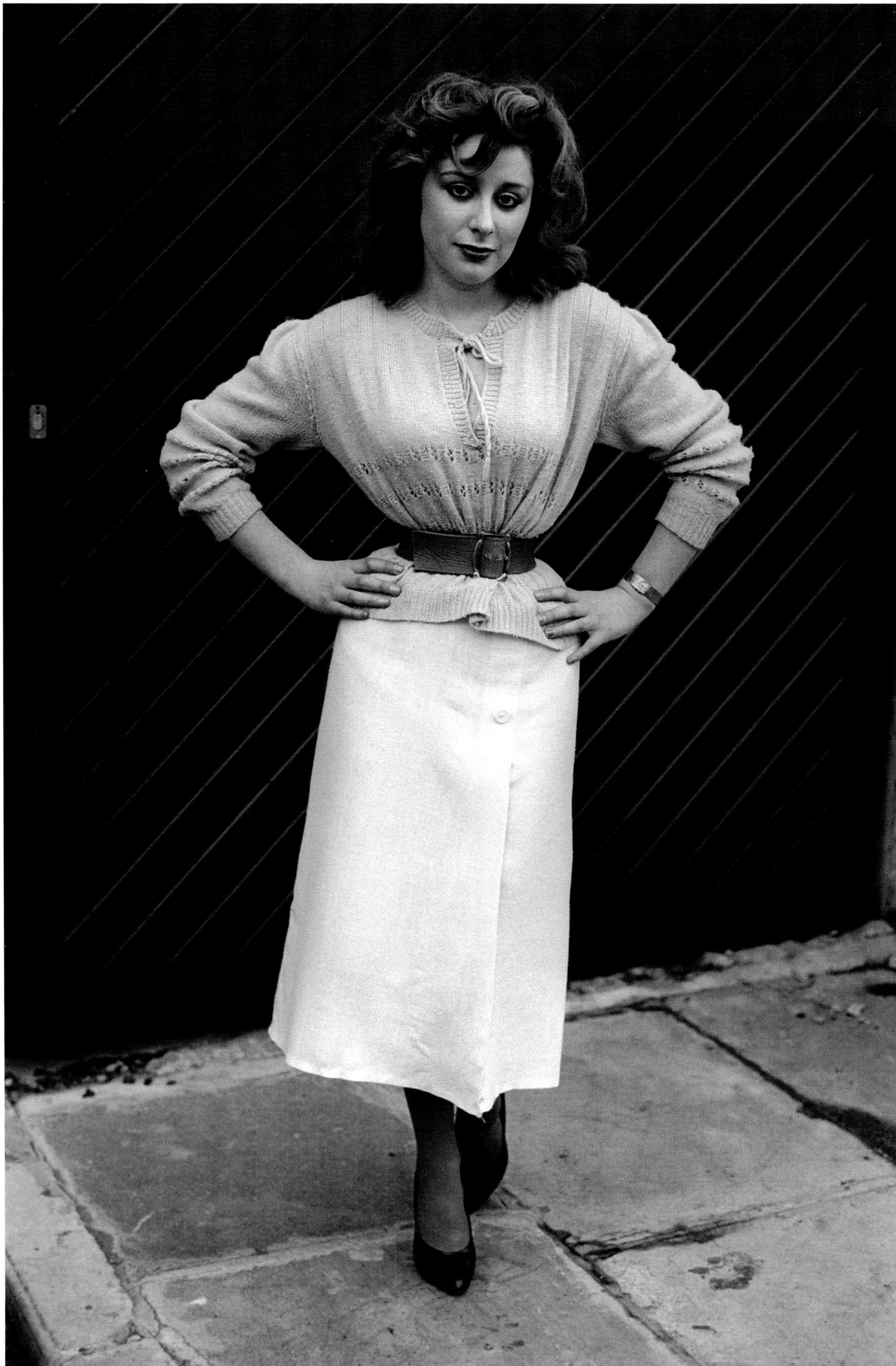

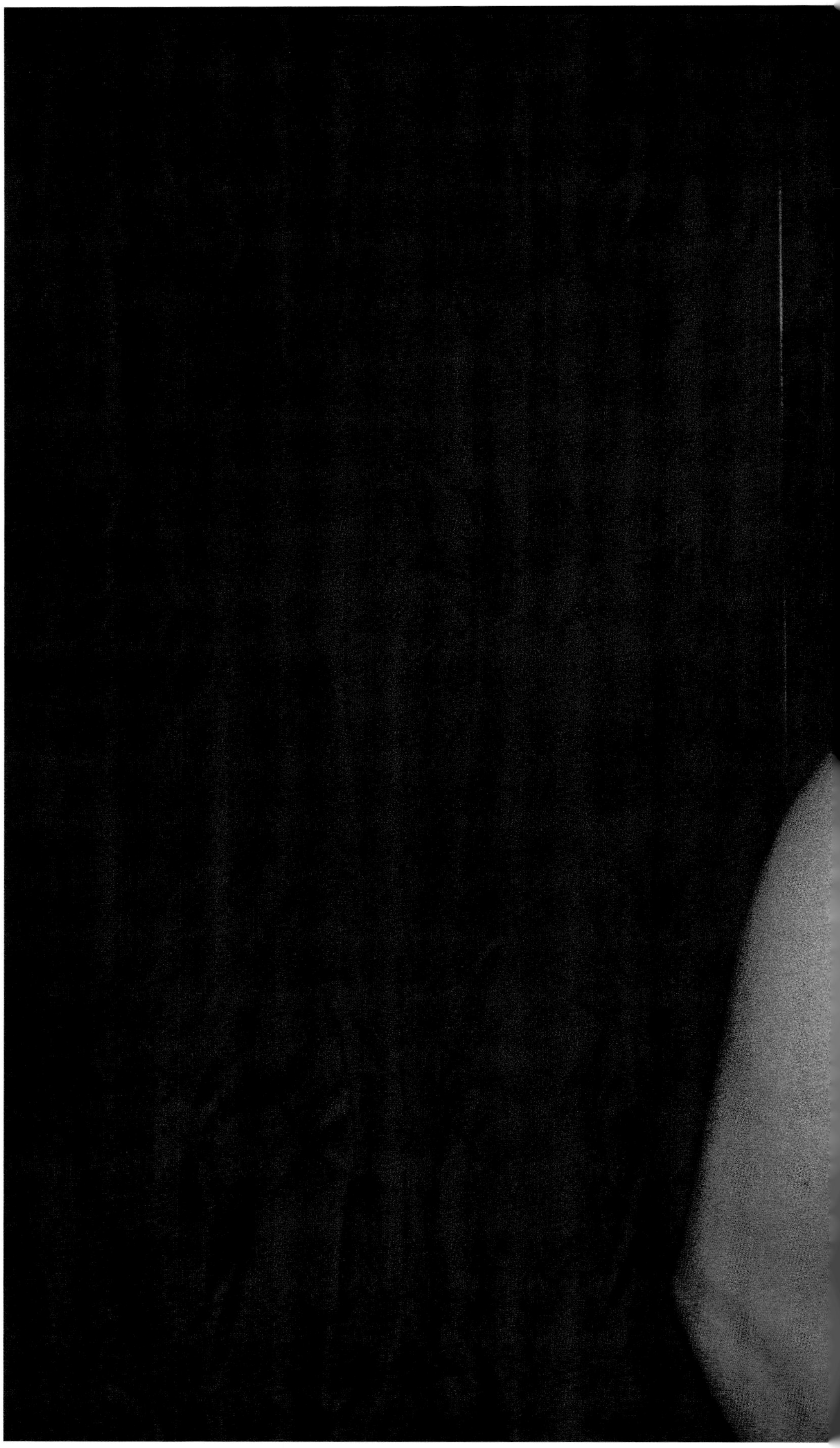

Kim, Planets,
Mayfair 1981.

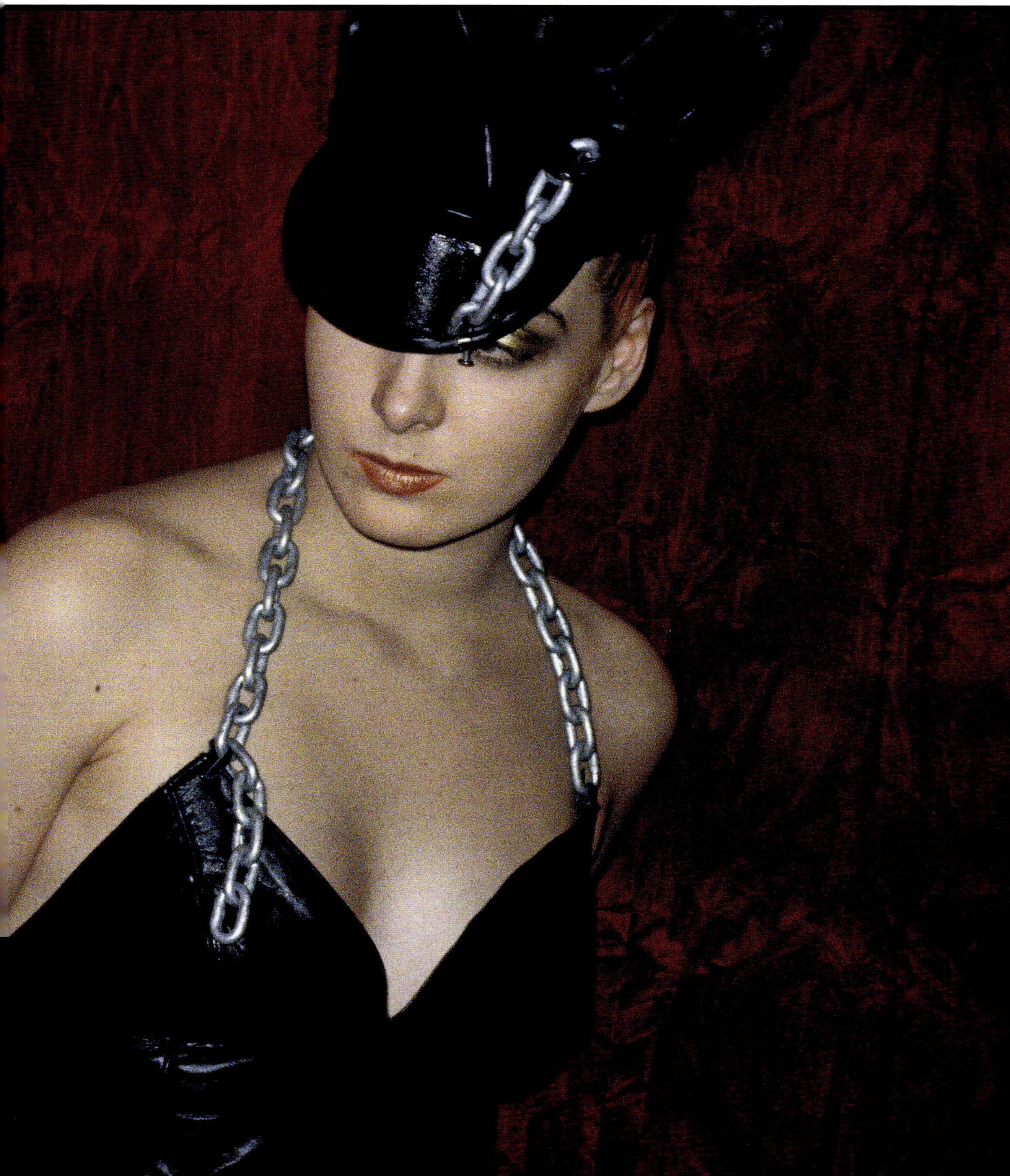

Jock & Fiona, Mayfair 1983.

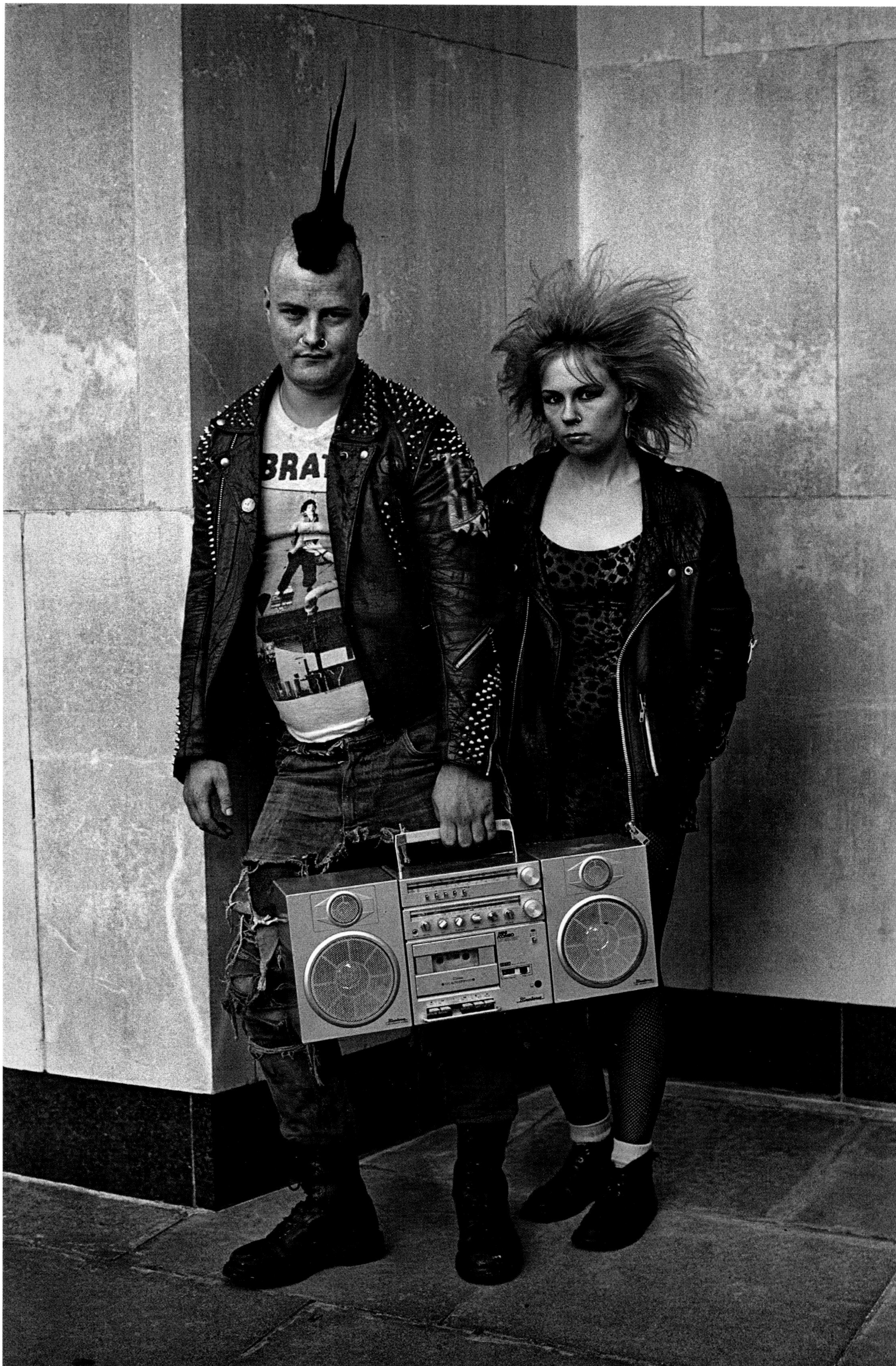

Name unknown, Camden Palace 1984.

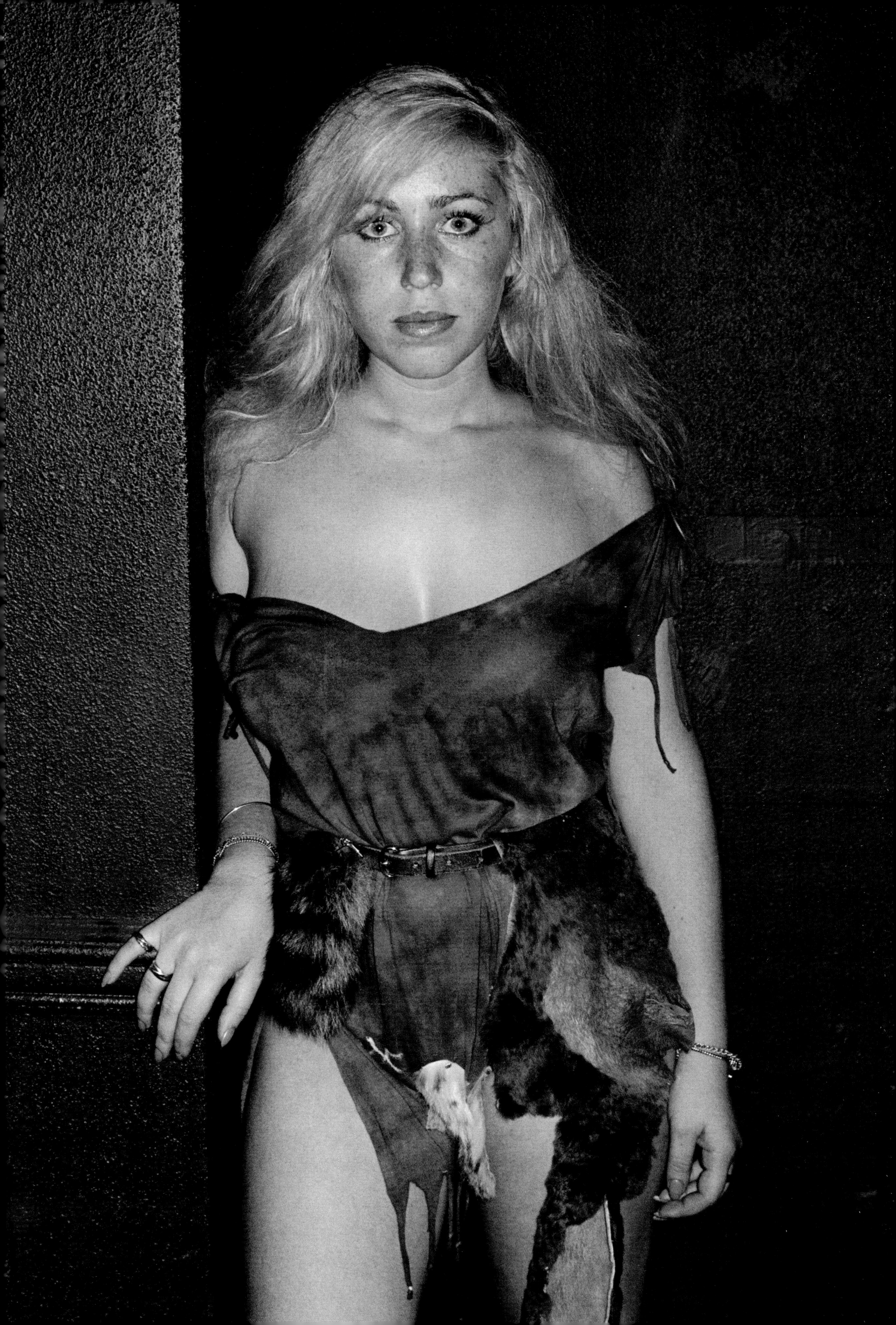

Name unkown, Portobello Road 1981.

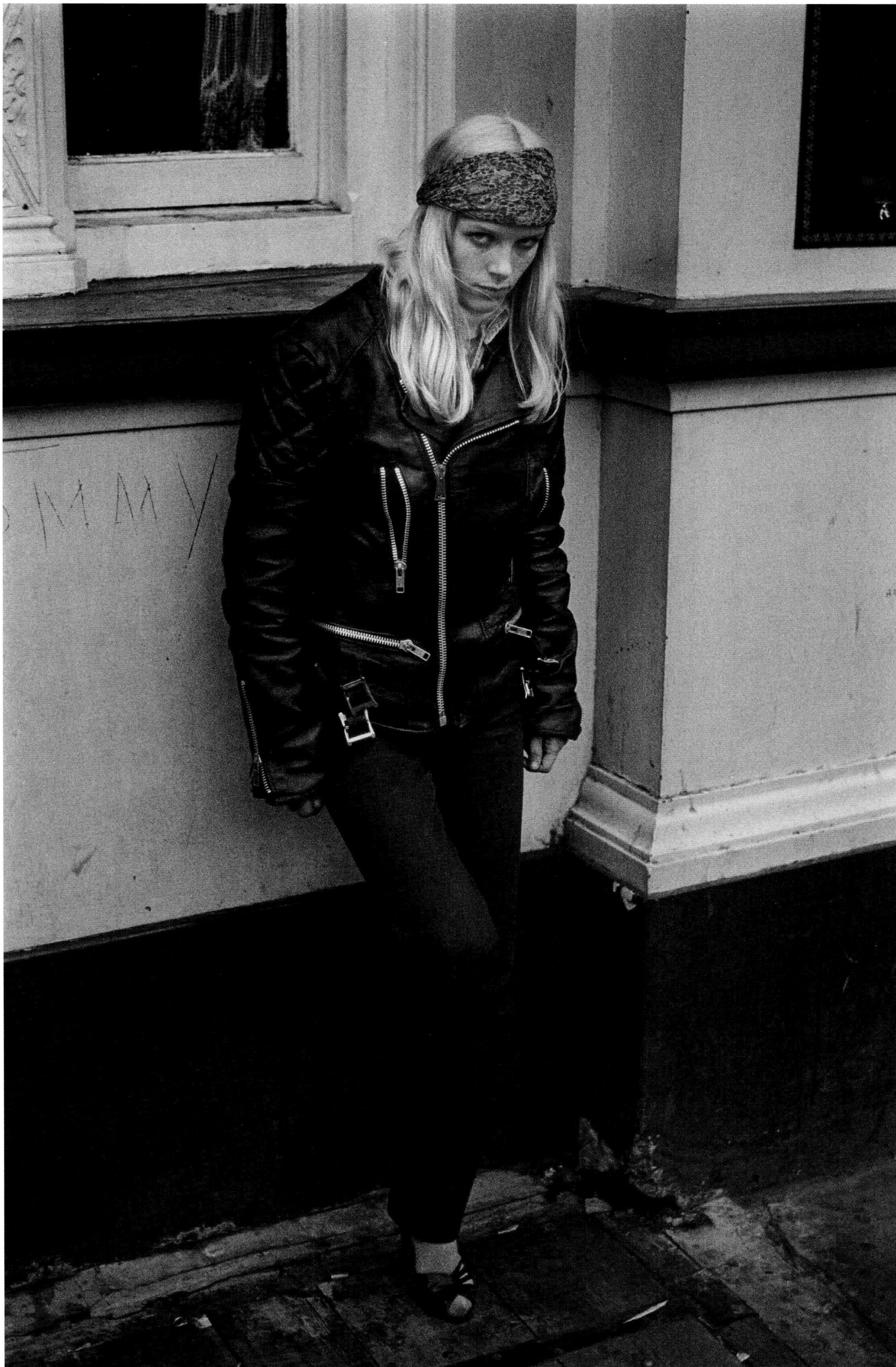

Lita, King's Road, Chelsea 1984.

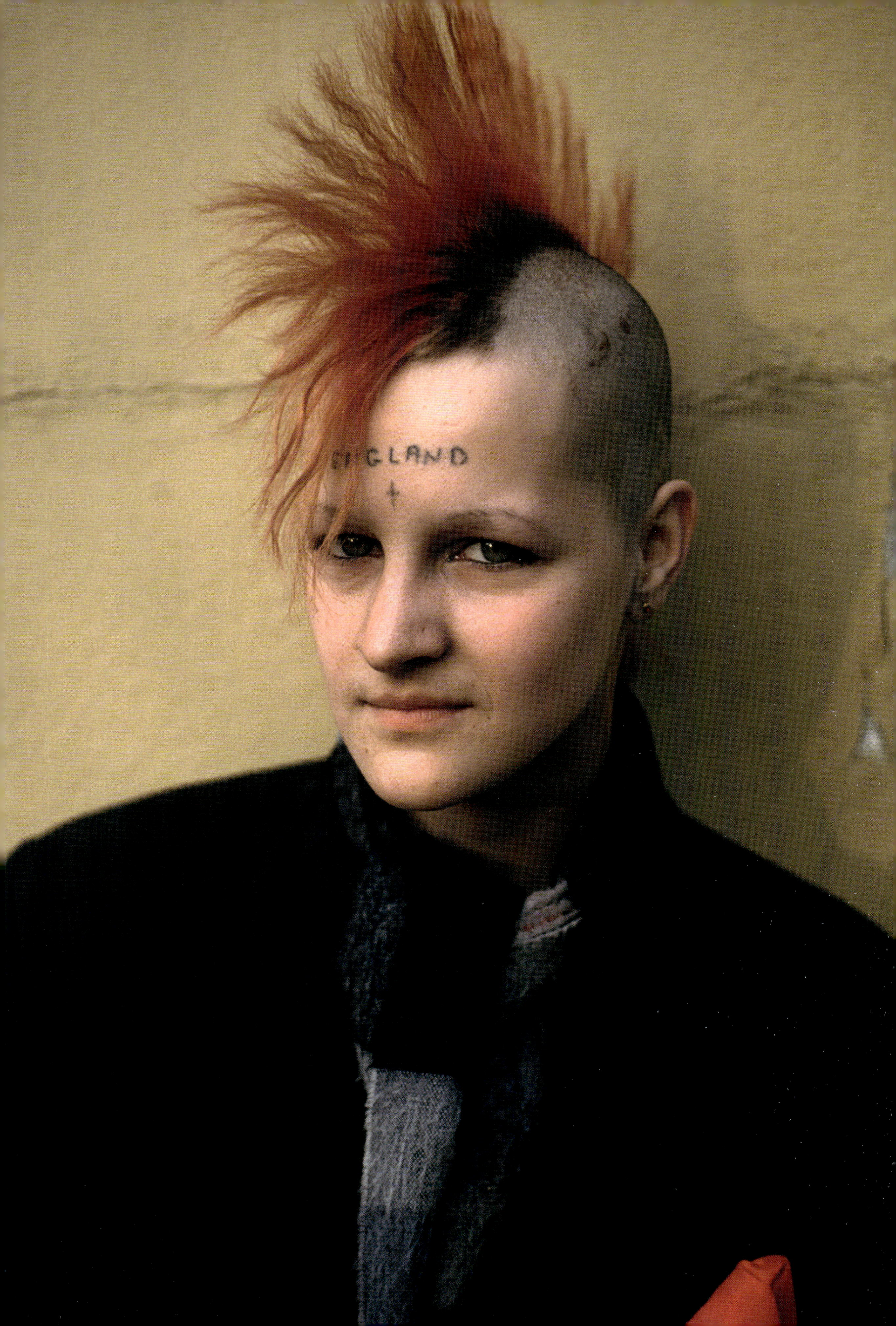

Dave, King's Road, Chelsea 1985.

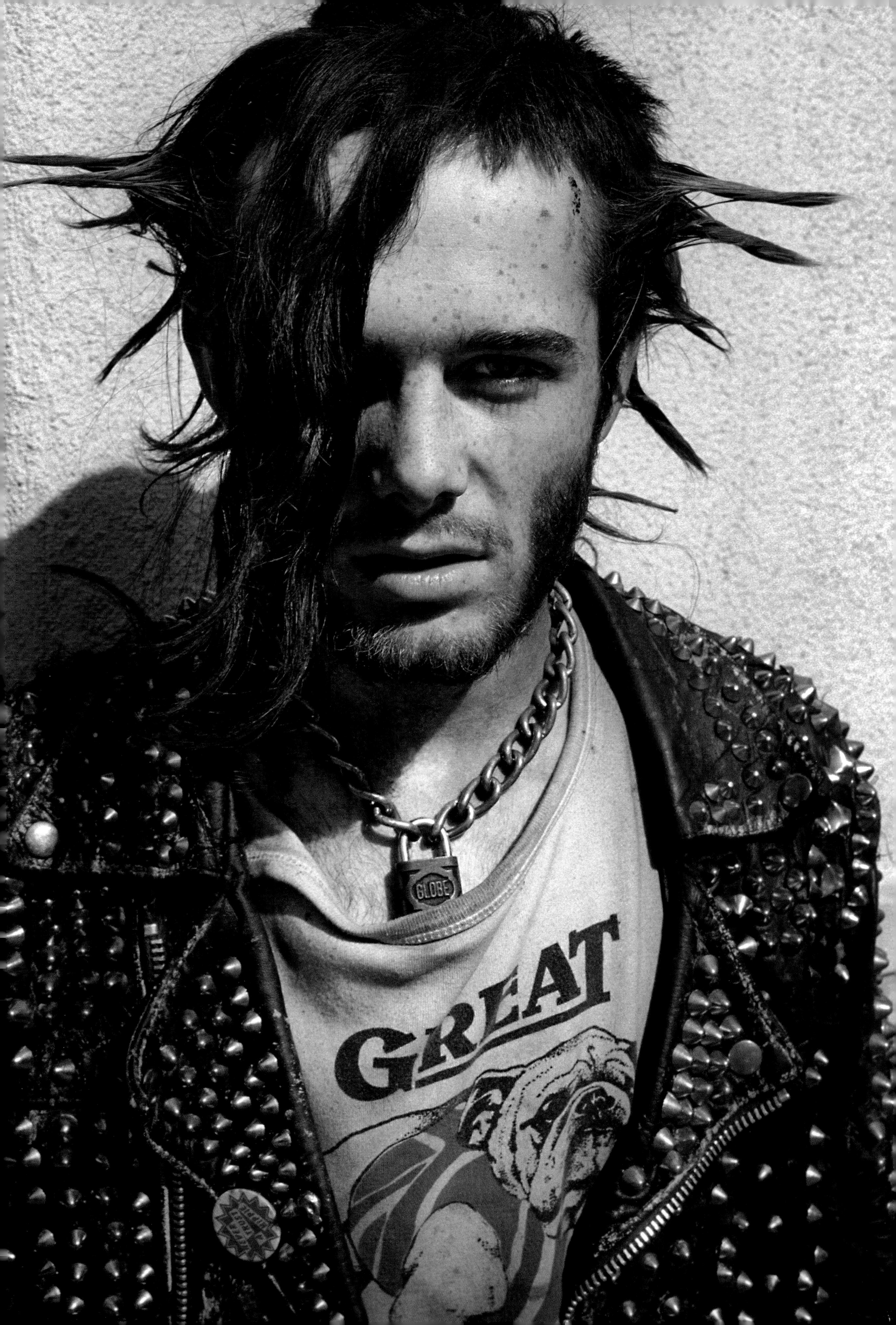
GLOBE
GREAT

Lemmy, King's Road, Chelsea 1982.

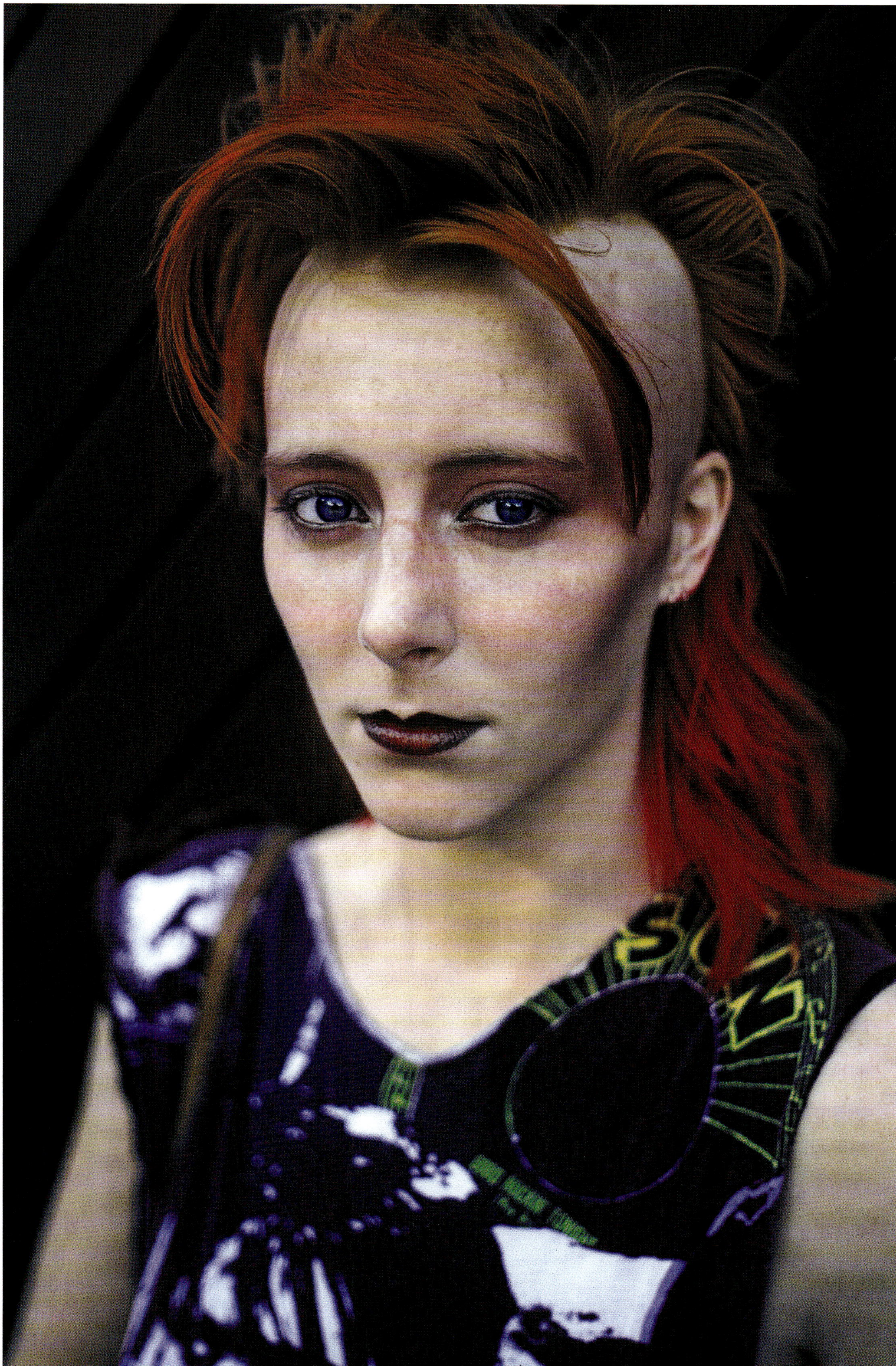

Martin & Scarlett, Camden Palace 1982.

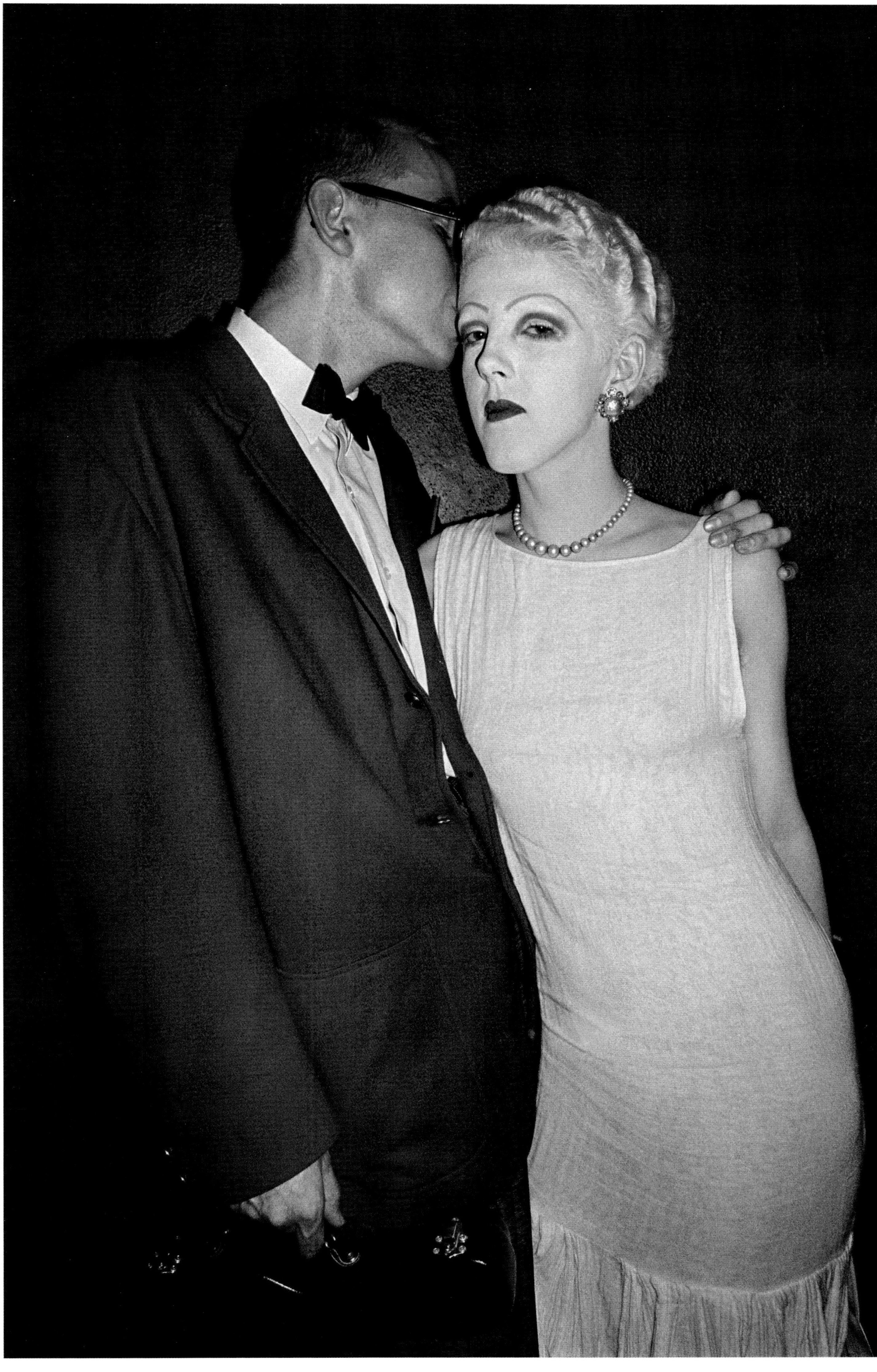

Flanagan, King's Road, Chelsea 1983.

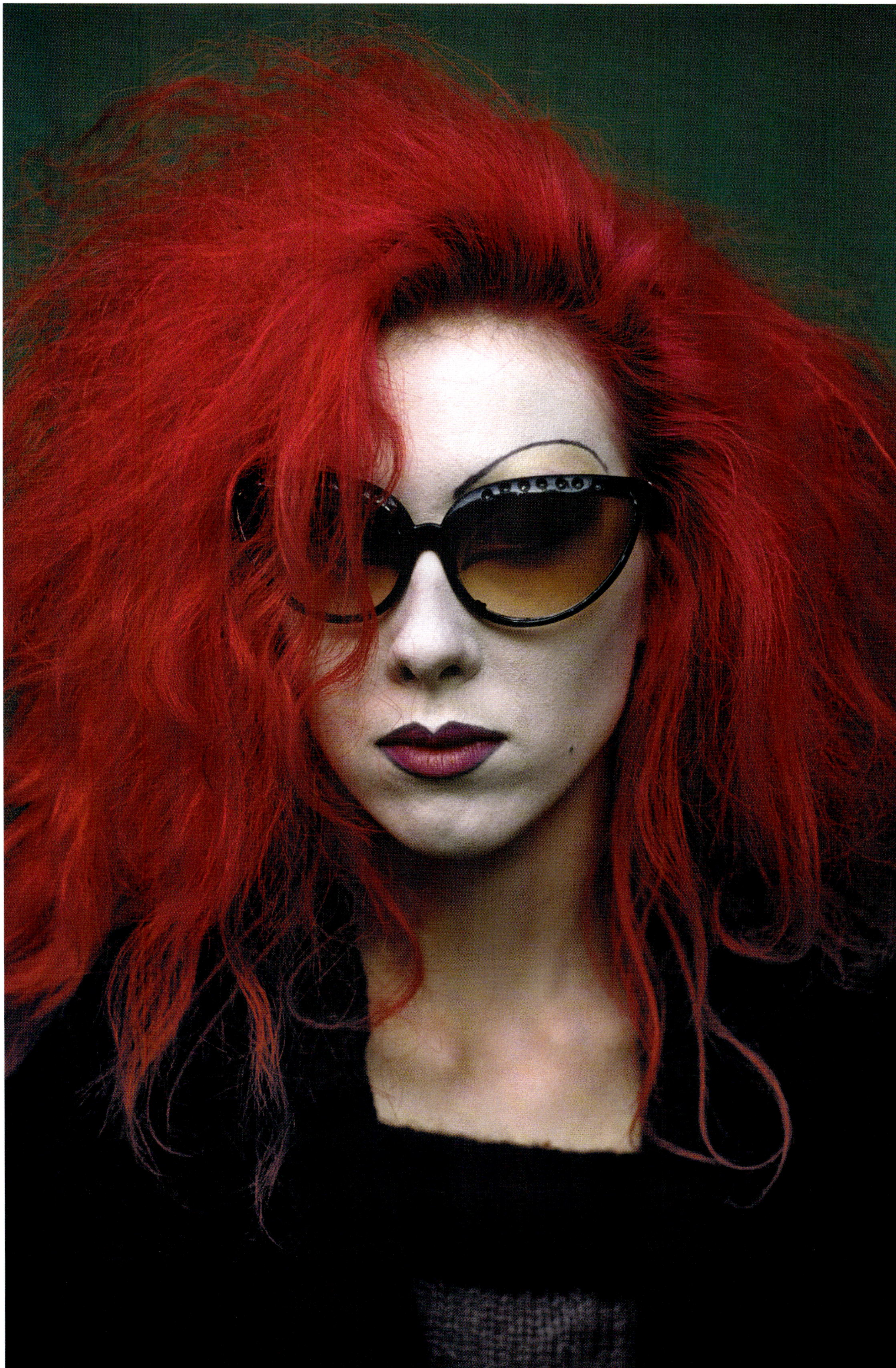

Wayne aka Smiler, Soho 1984.

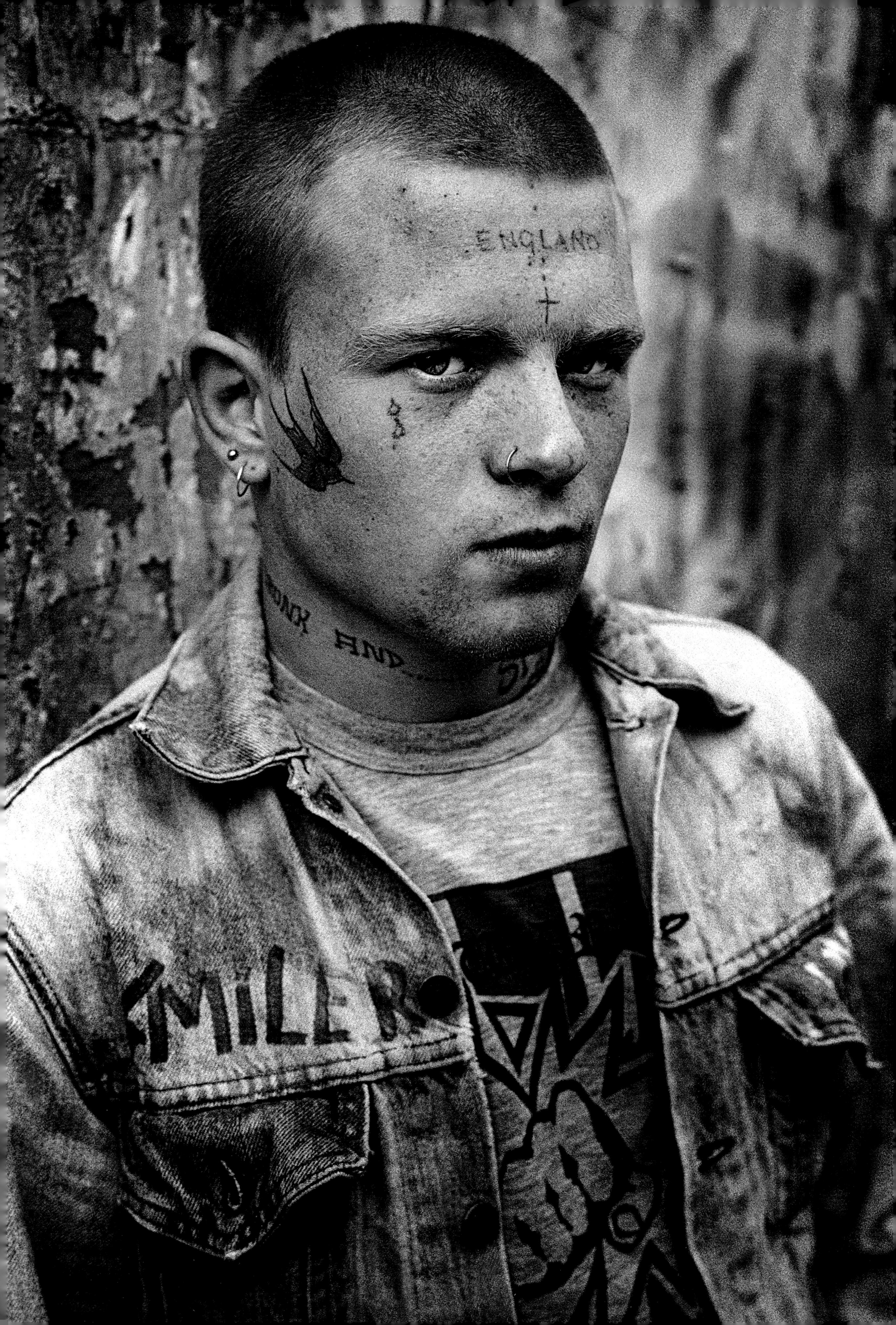
ENGLAND

Name unknown, Sacrosanct, Shaftesbury Avenue 1985.

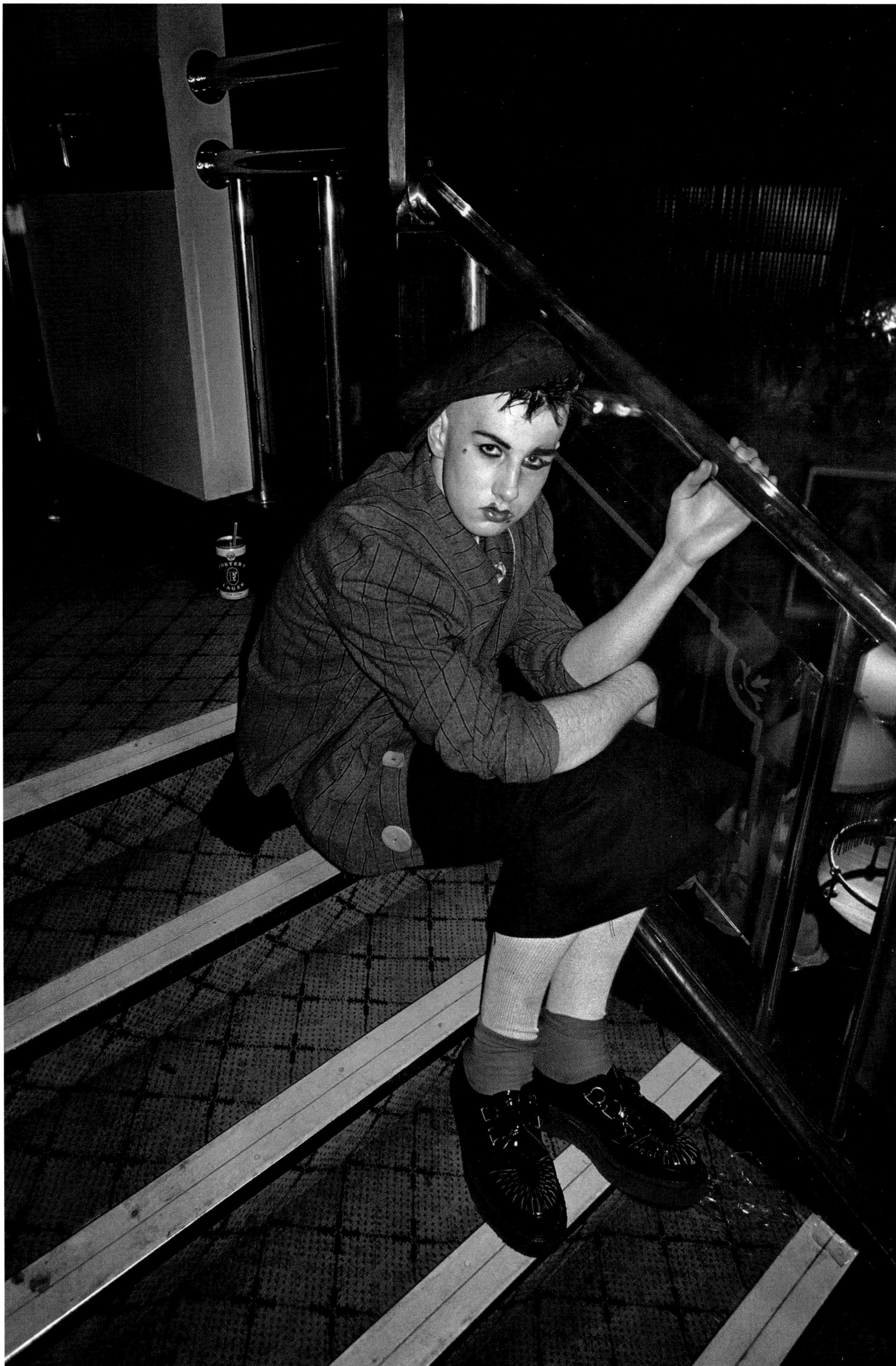

Scarlett, Chelsea 1983.

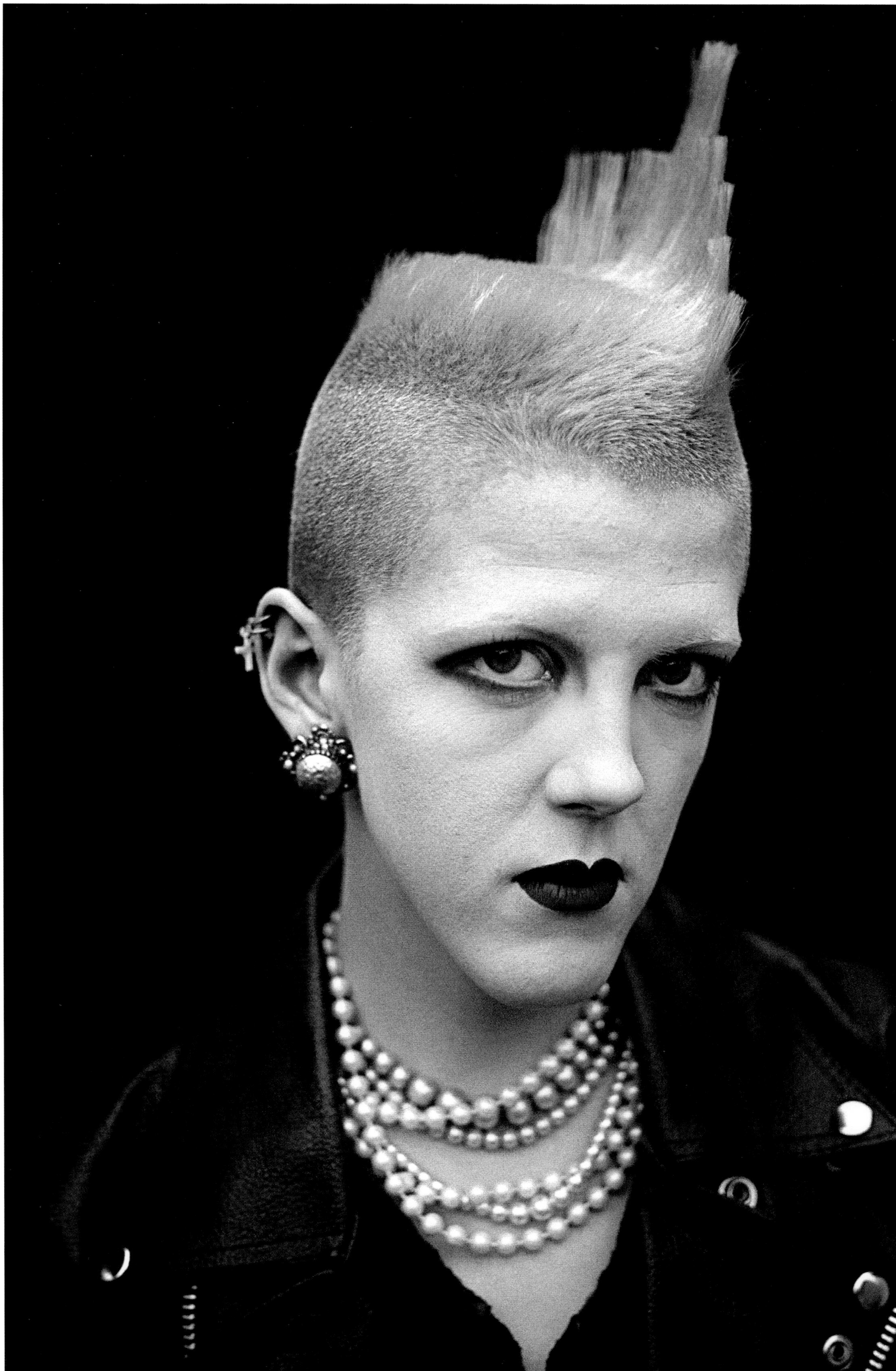

Tanya, The Batcave 1983.

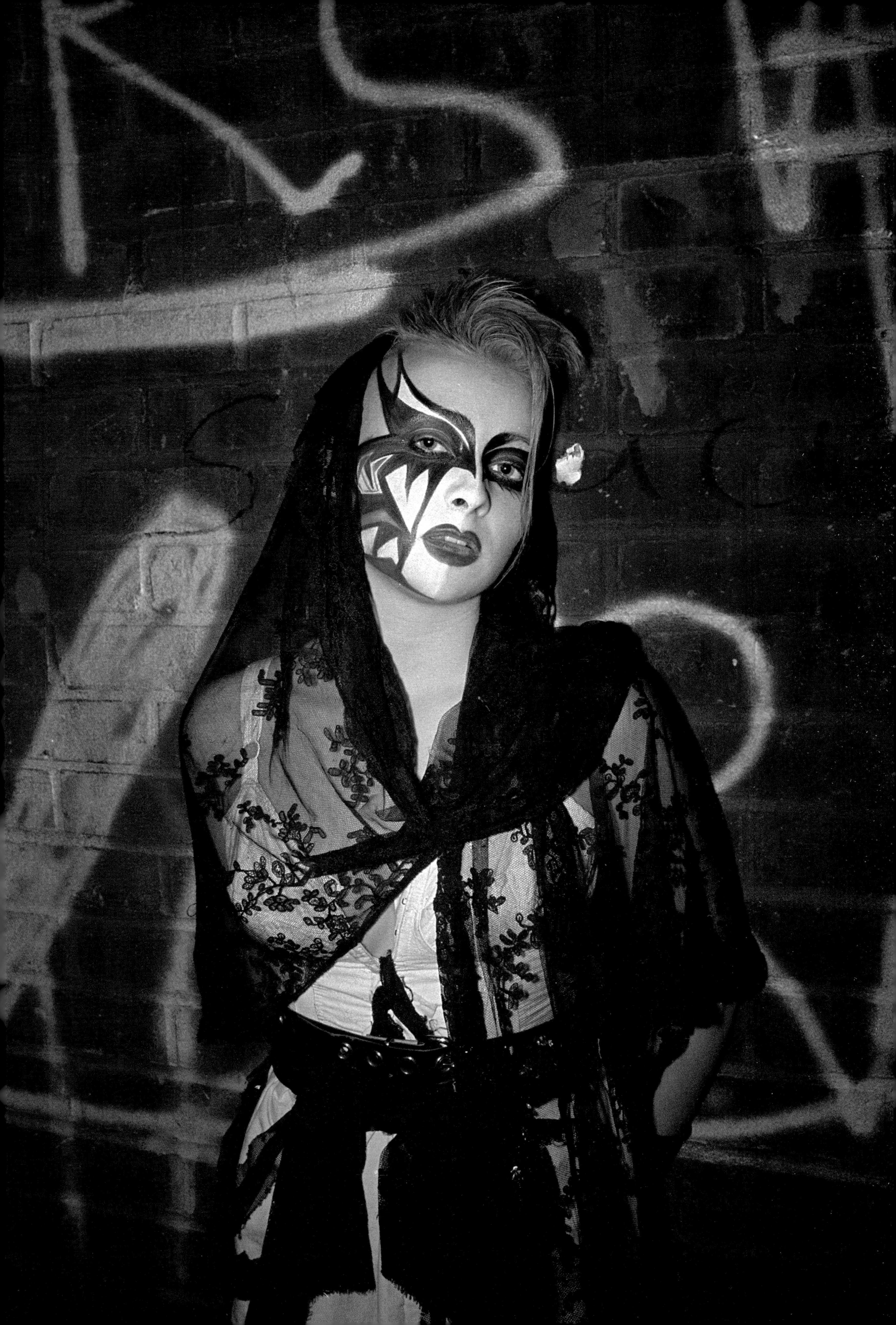

Caroline, Skin Two, Soho 1983.

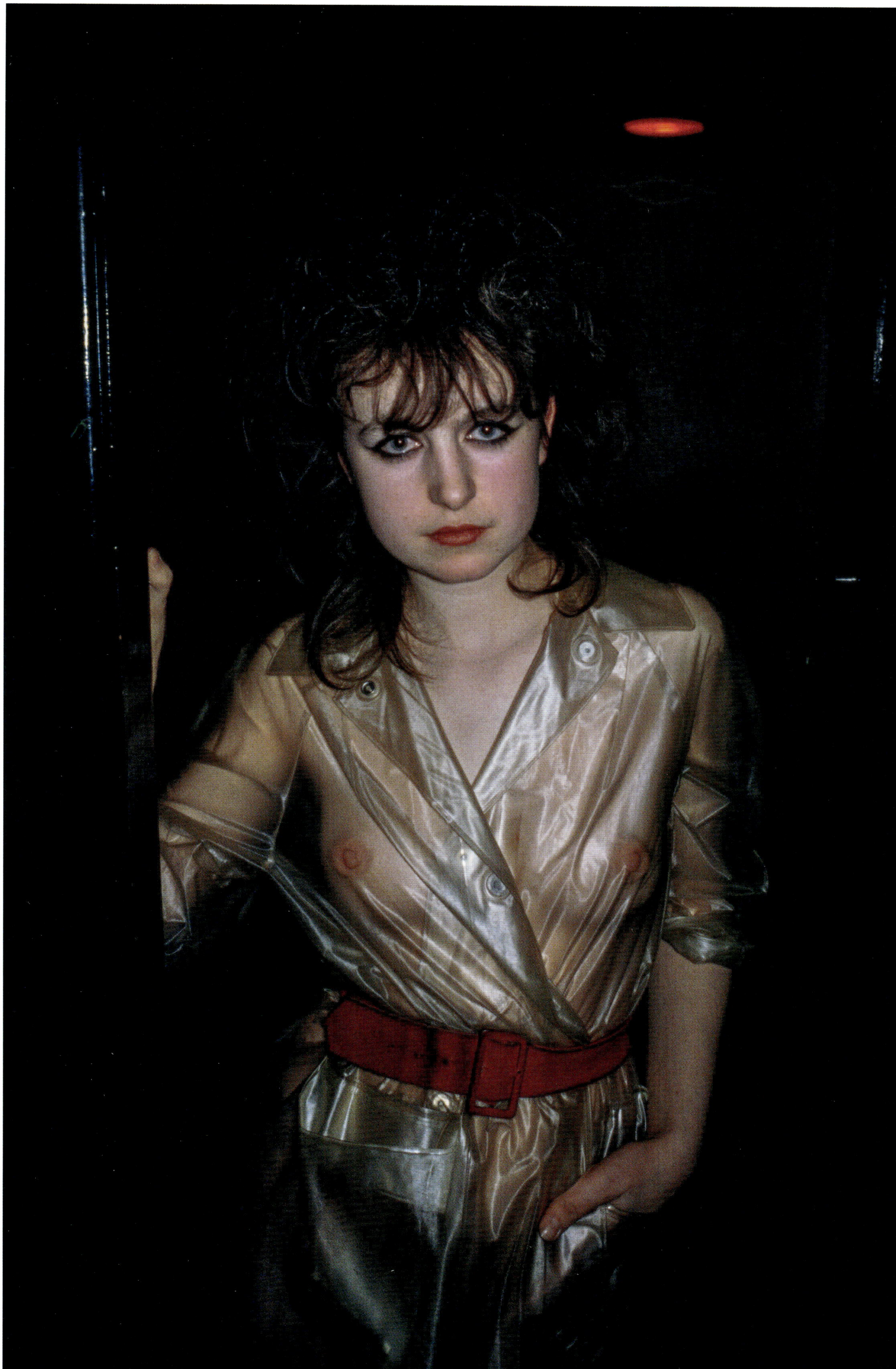

Sharon, Brixton 1983.

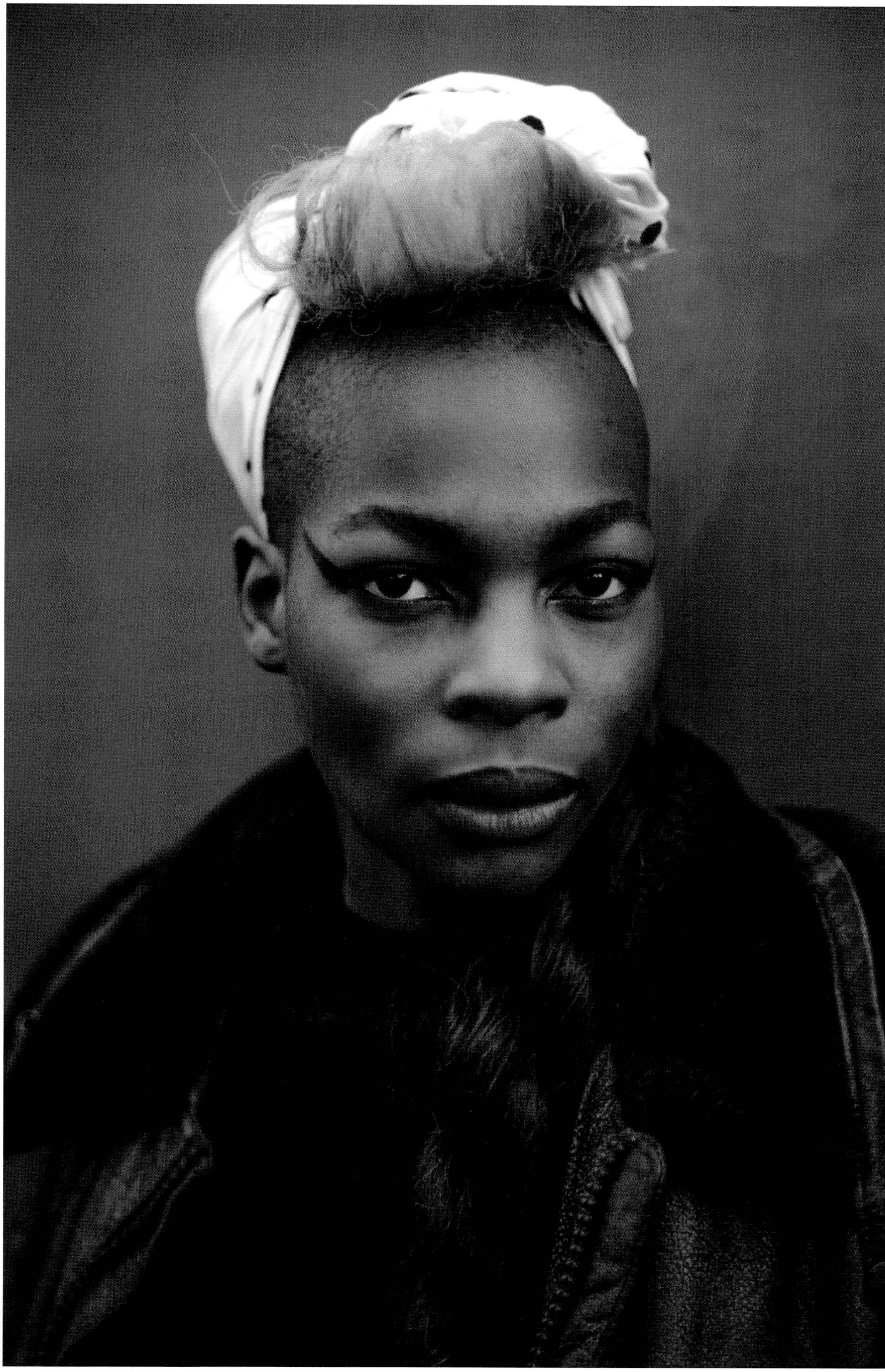

Name unknown, Portobello Road 1983.

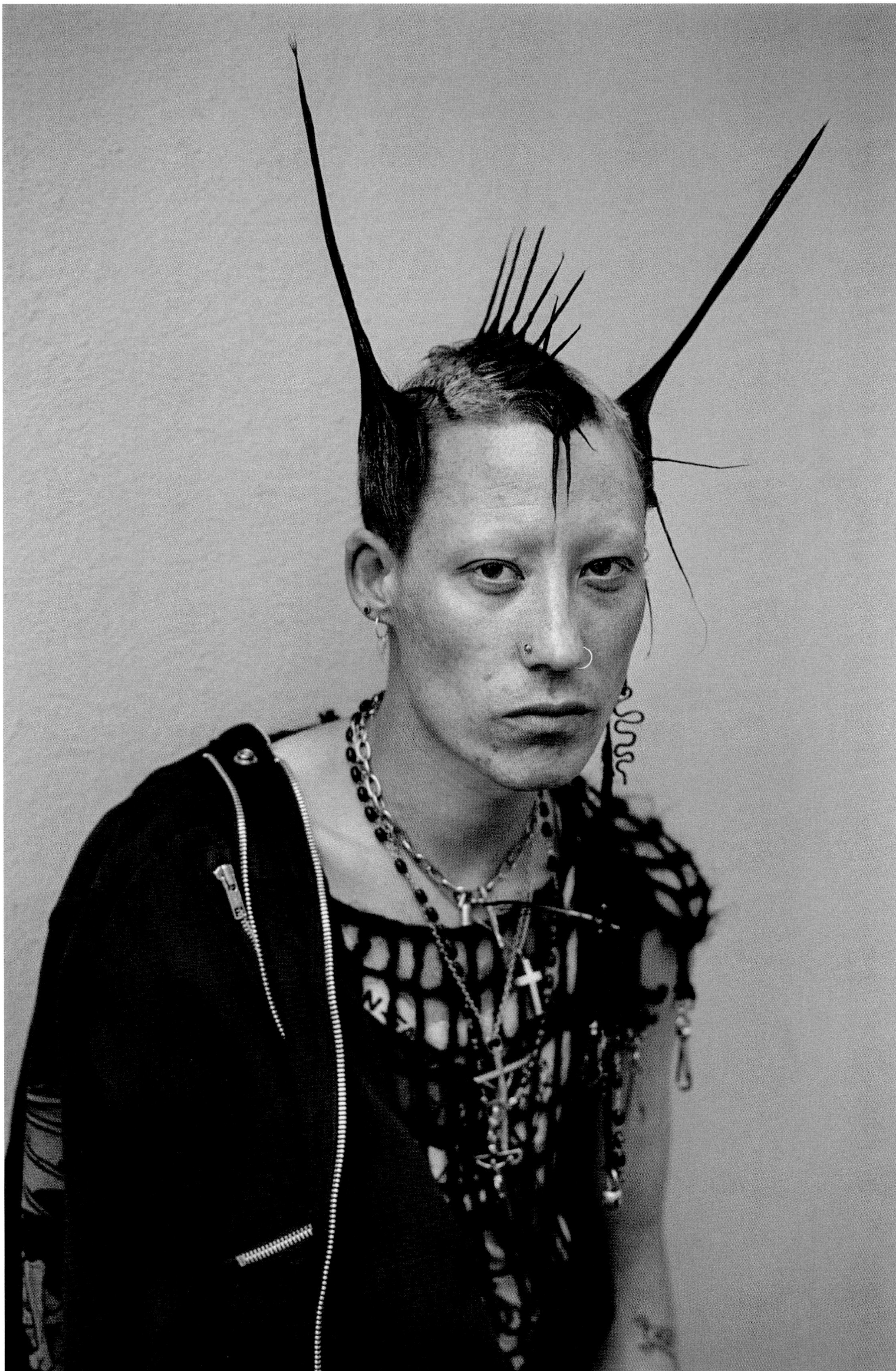

Kevin, Goulston Street, Aldgate 1981.

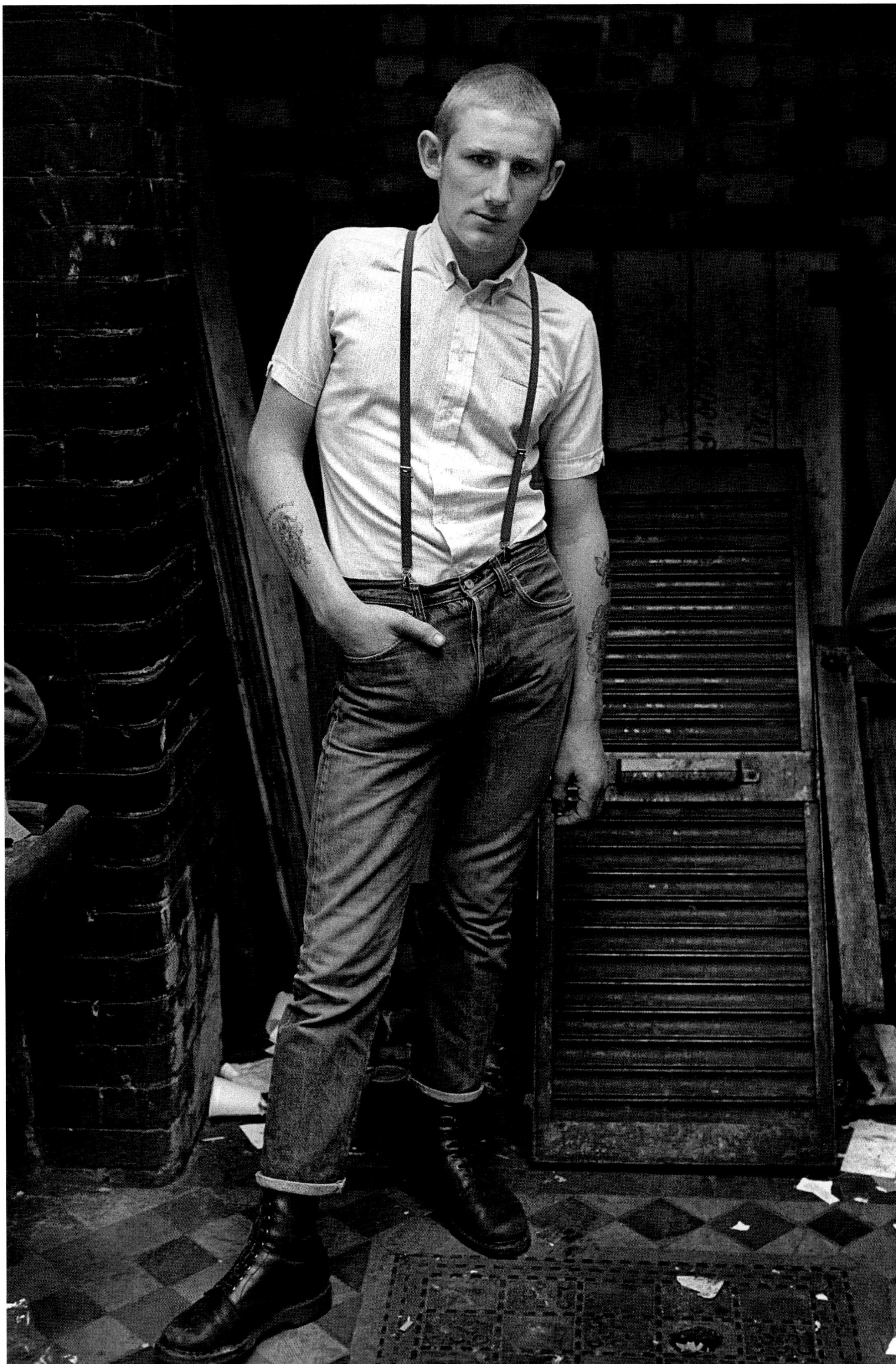

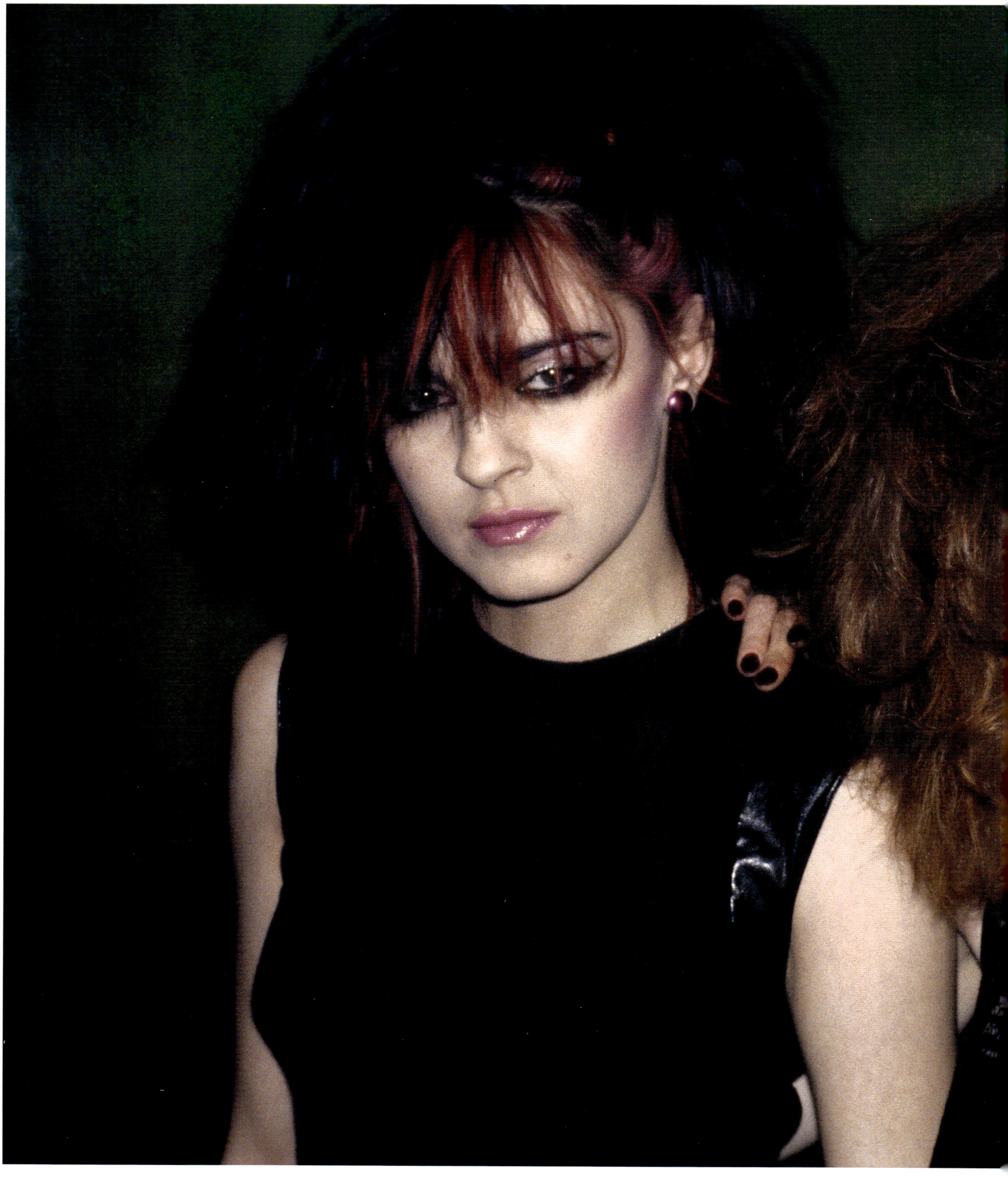

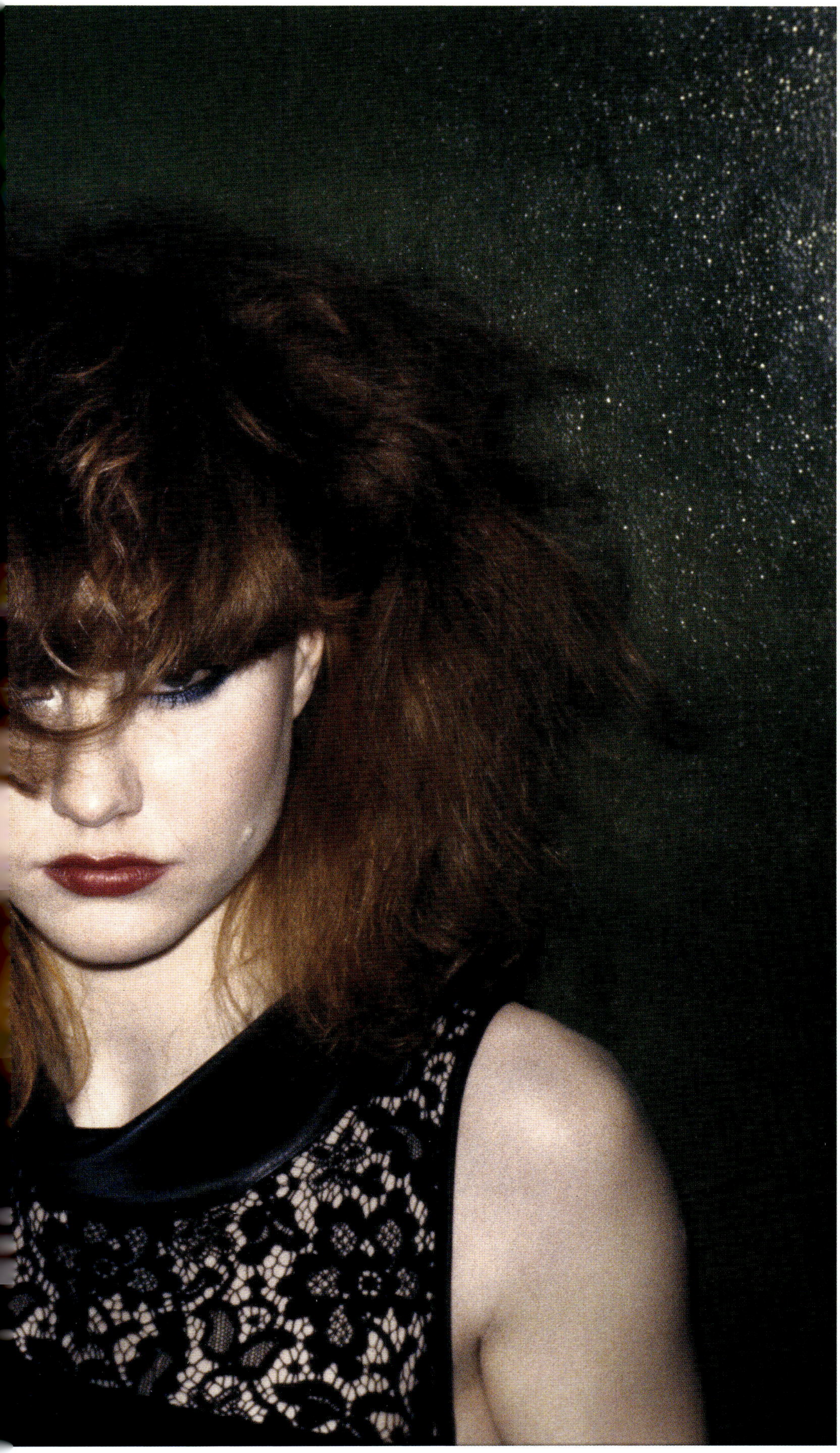

Wendy & Lorraine, Blitz, Covent Garden 1980.

Name unkown, near Carnaby Street 1980.

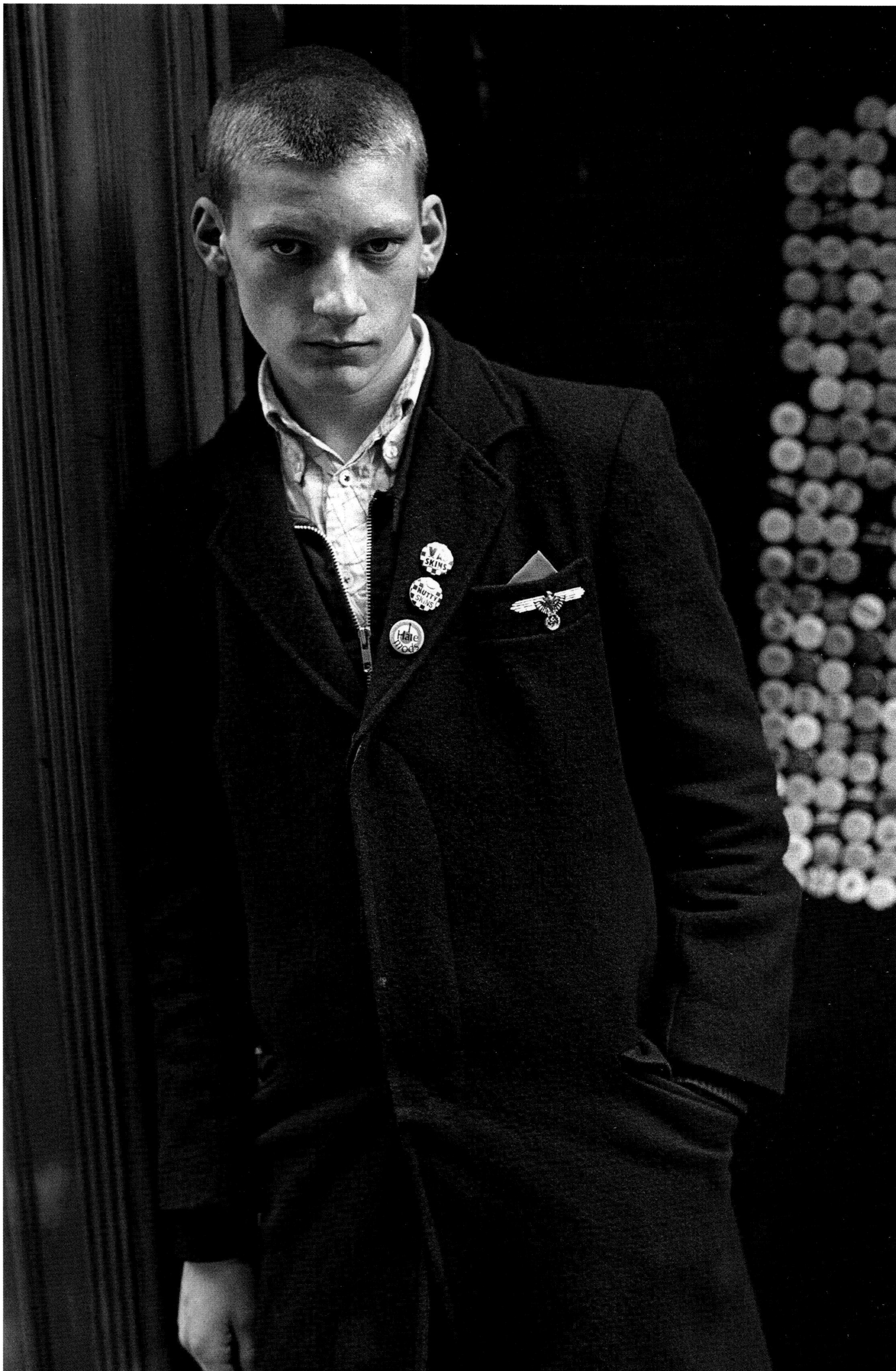
SKINS
NUTTY SKINS
I Hate mods

Crissi, King's Road, Chelsea 1983.

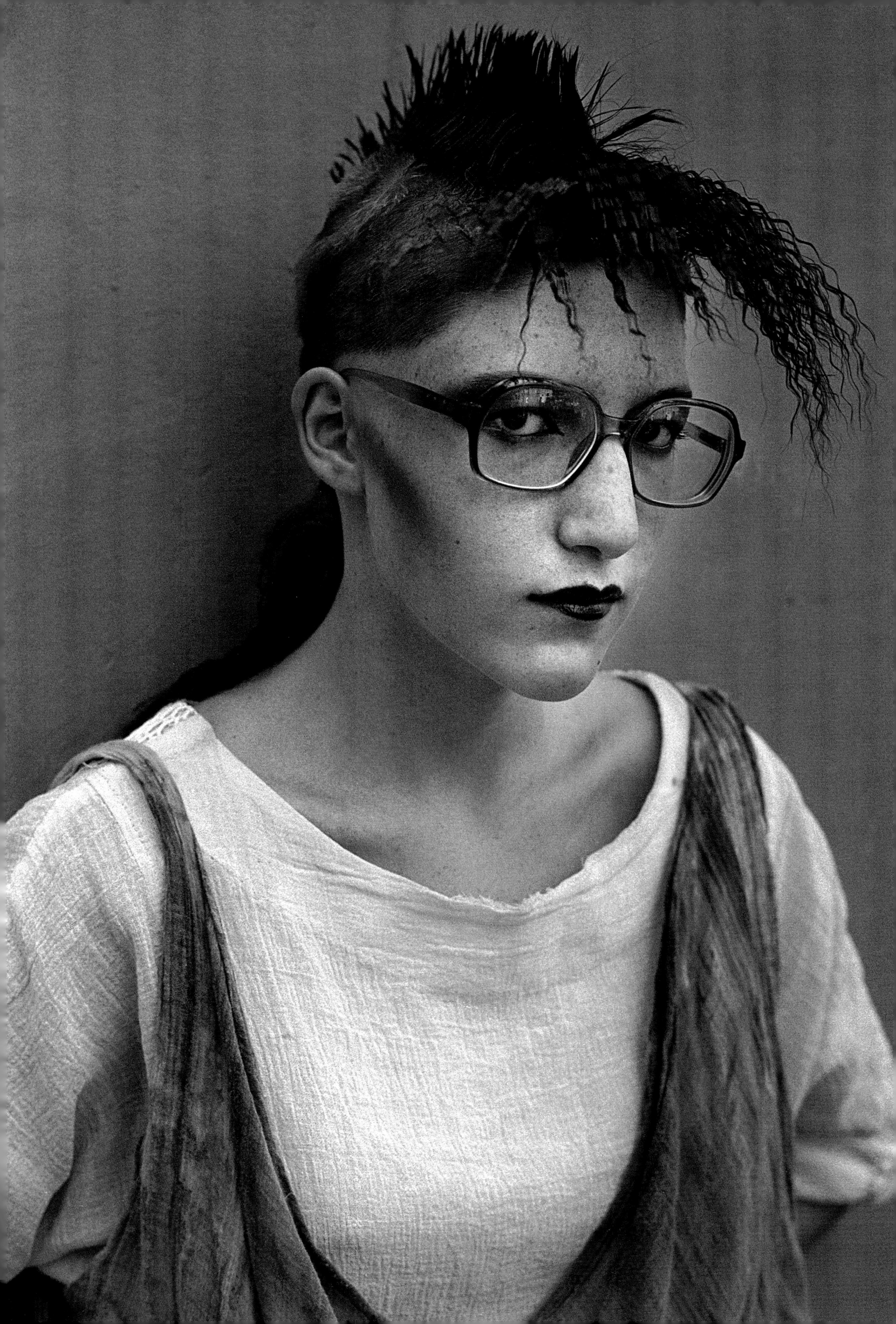

Dave, Brixton 1983.

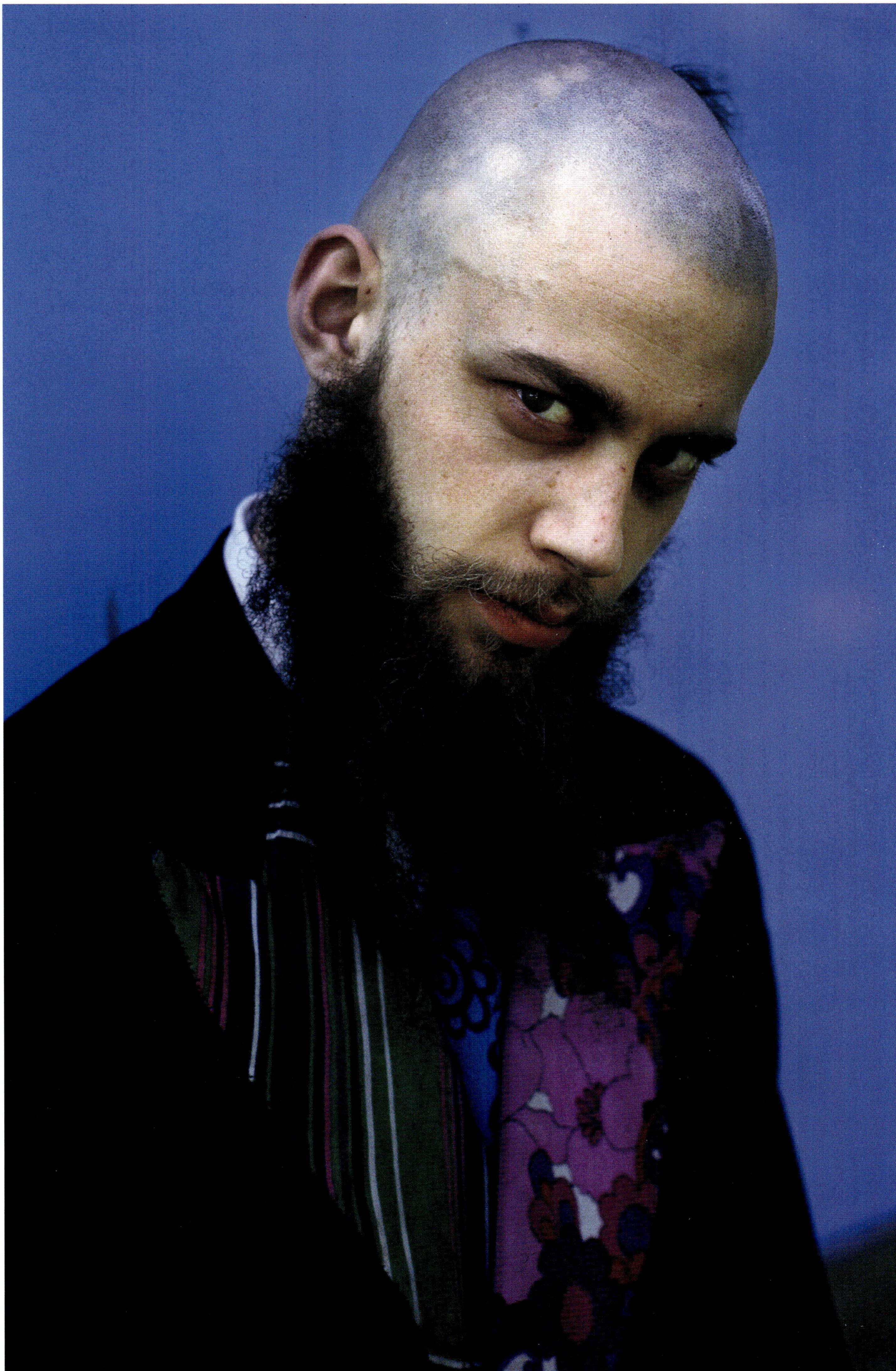

Mark, Taboo, Leicester Square 1985.

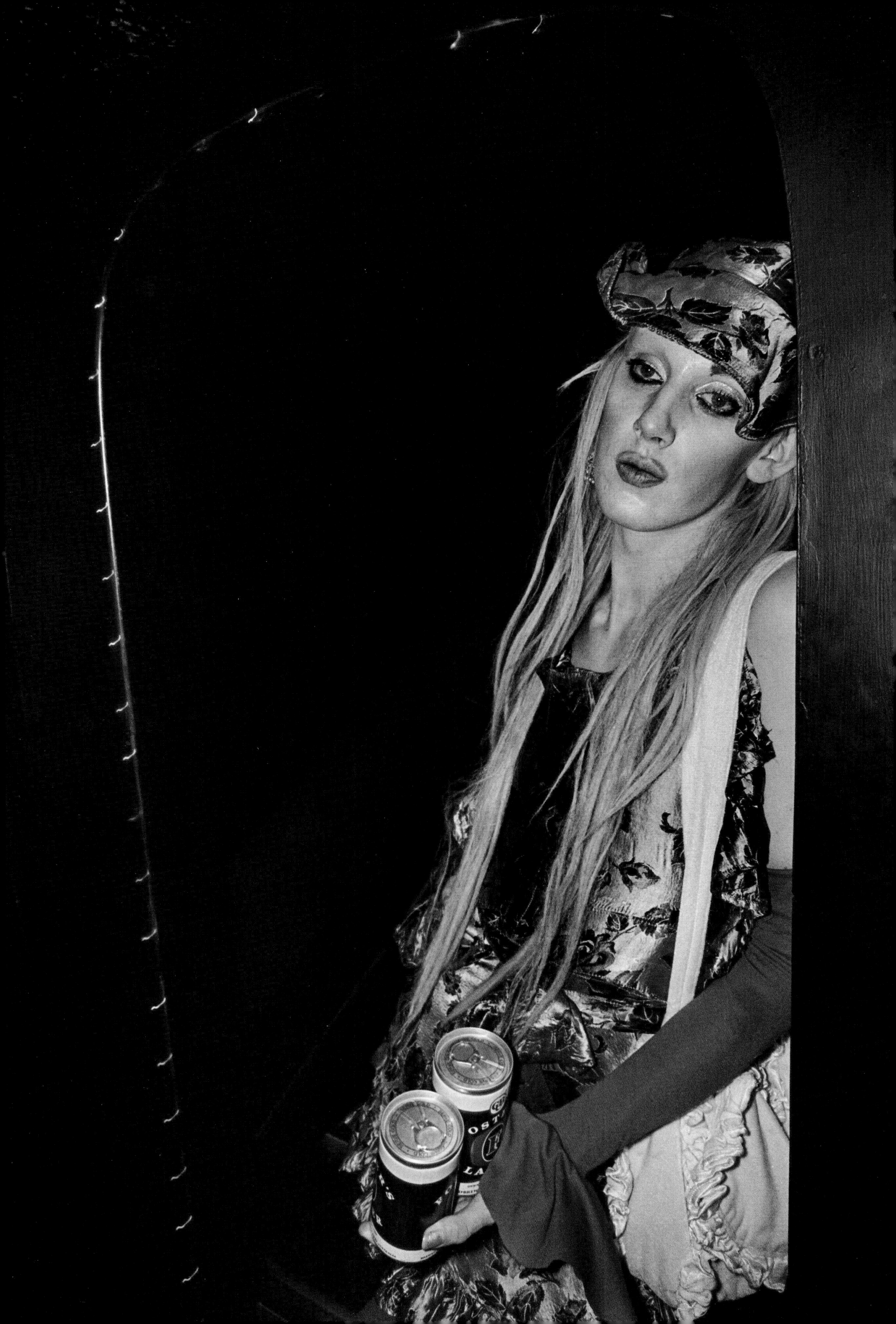

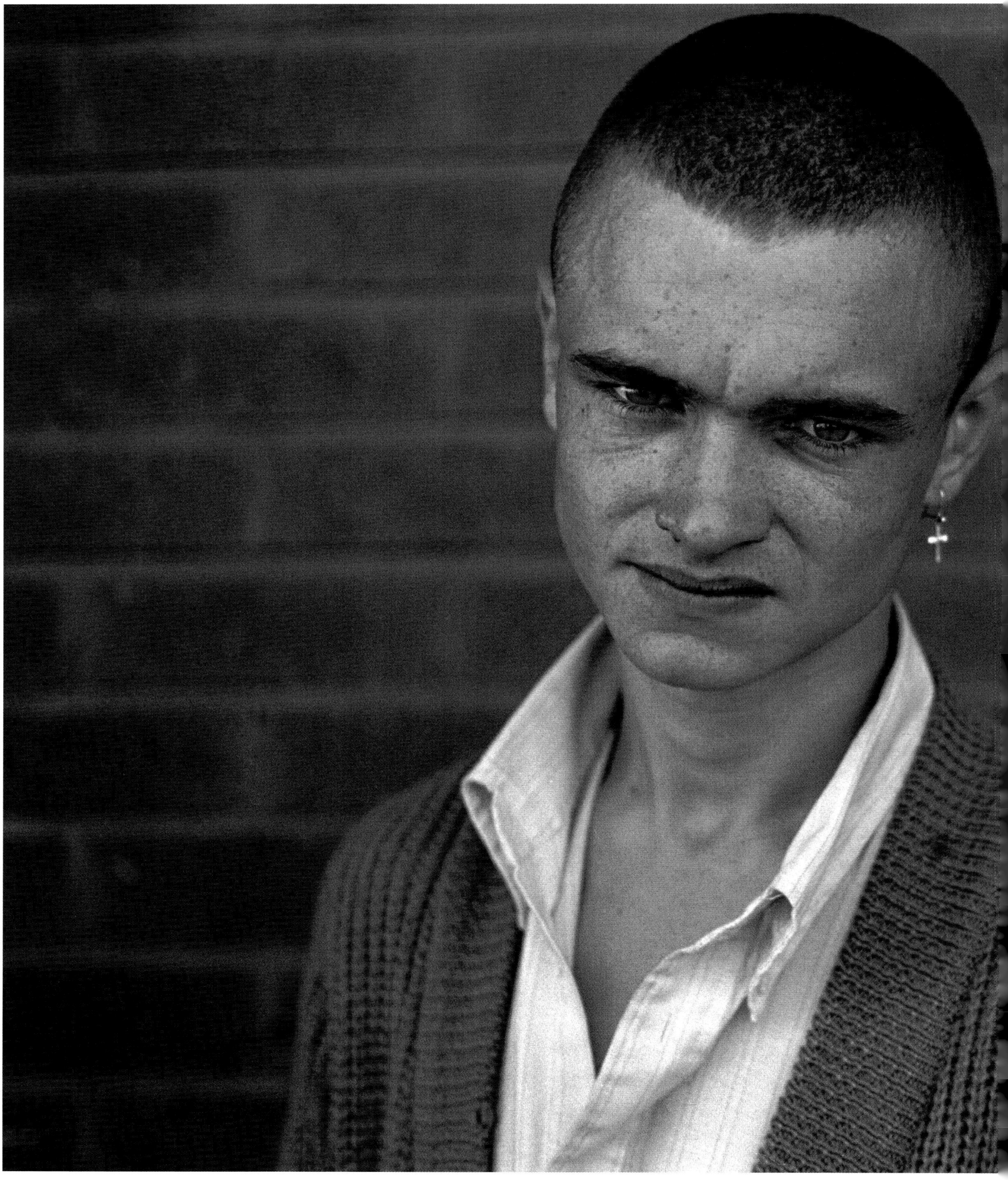

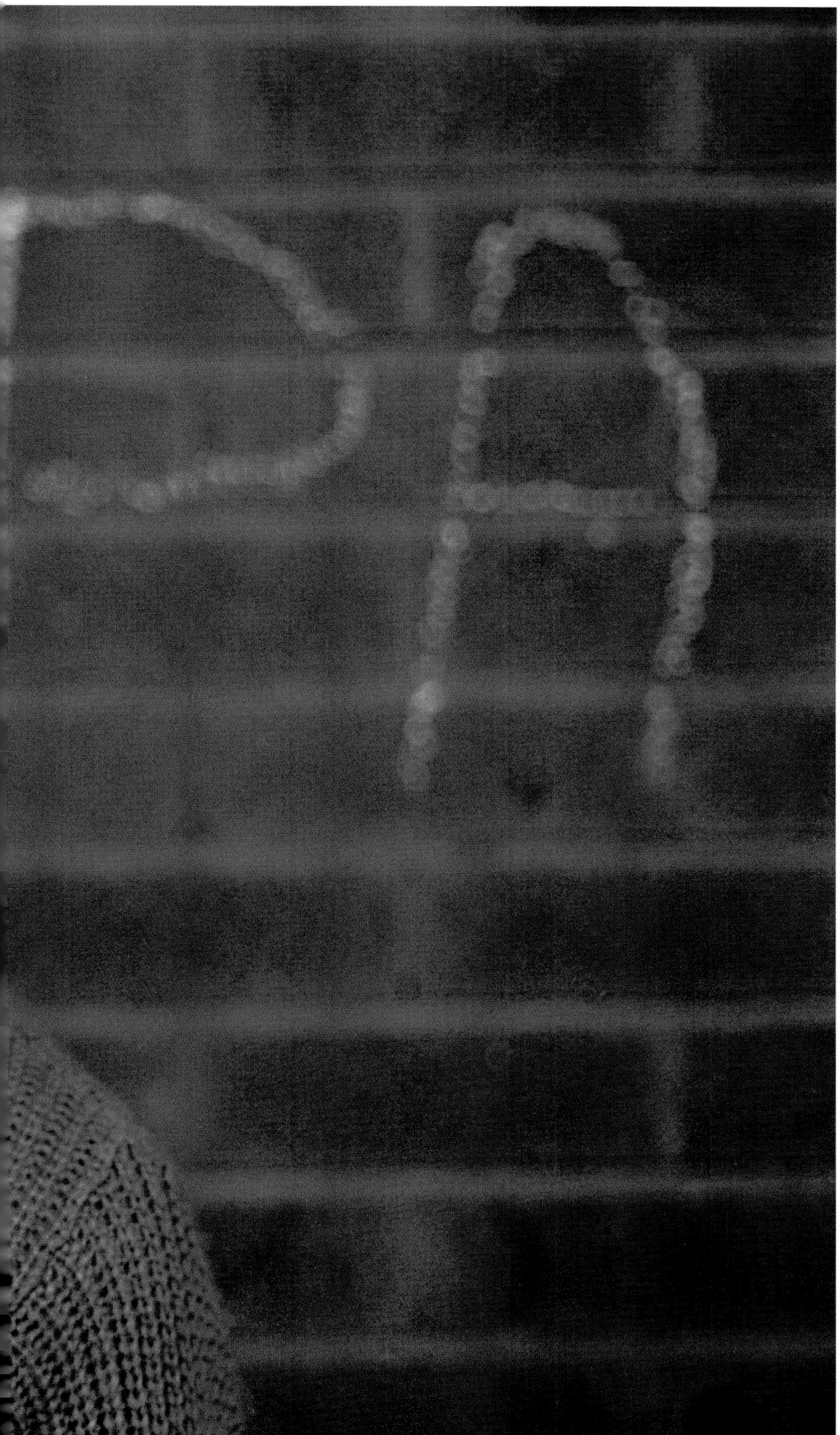

Name unknown,
Brighton 1980.

Lisa, Shaftesbury Avenue 1984.

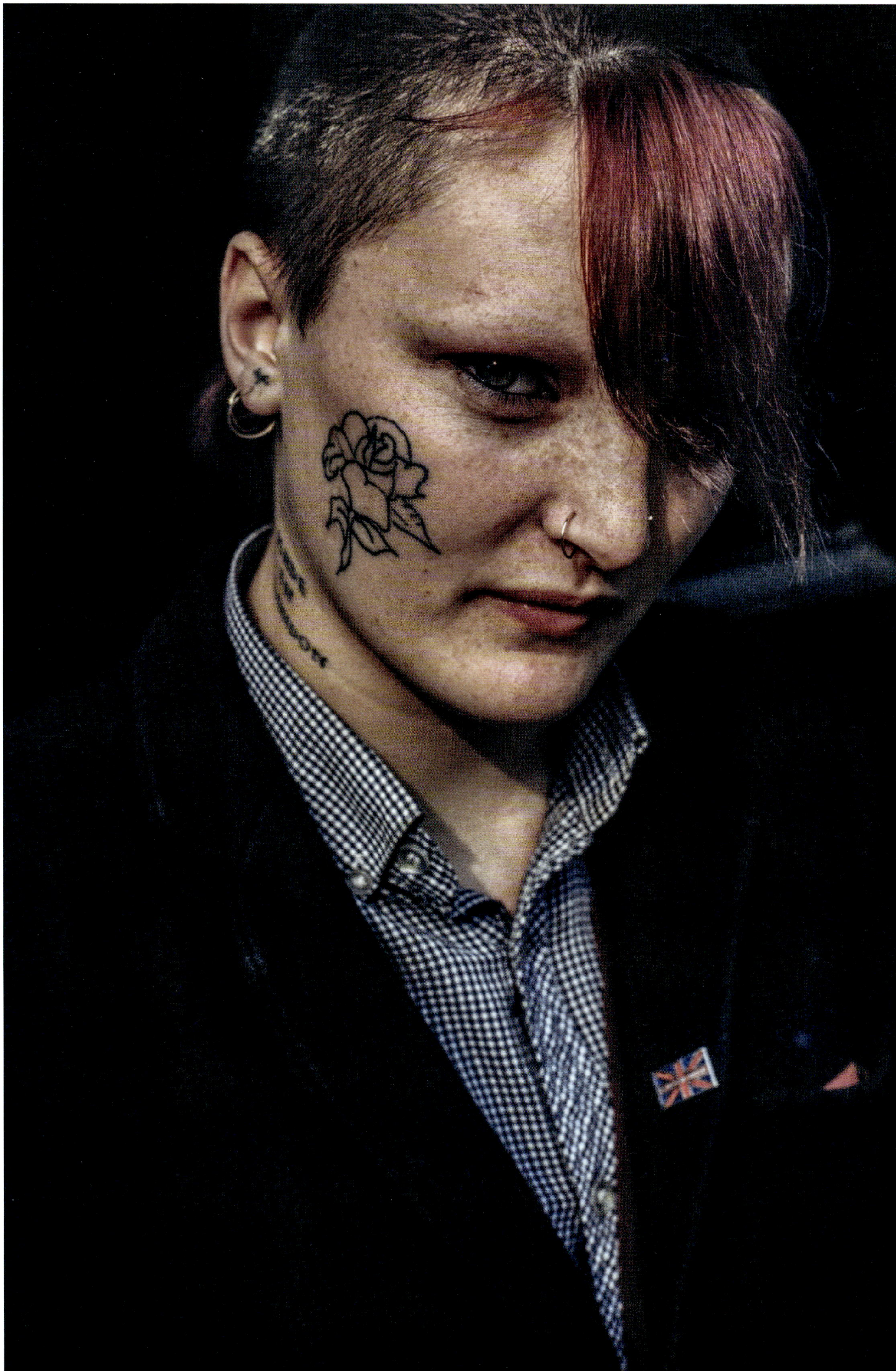

Name unknown, King's Road, Chelsea 1984.

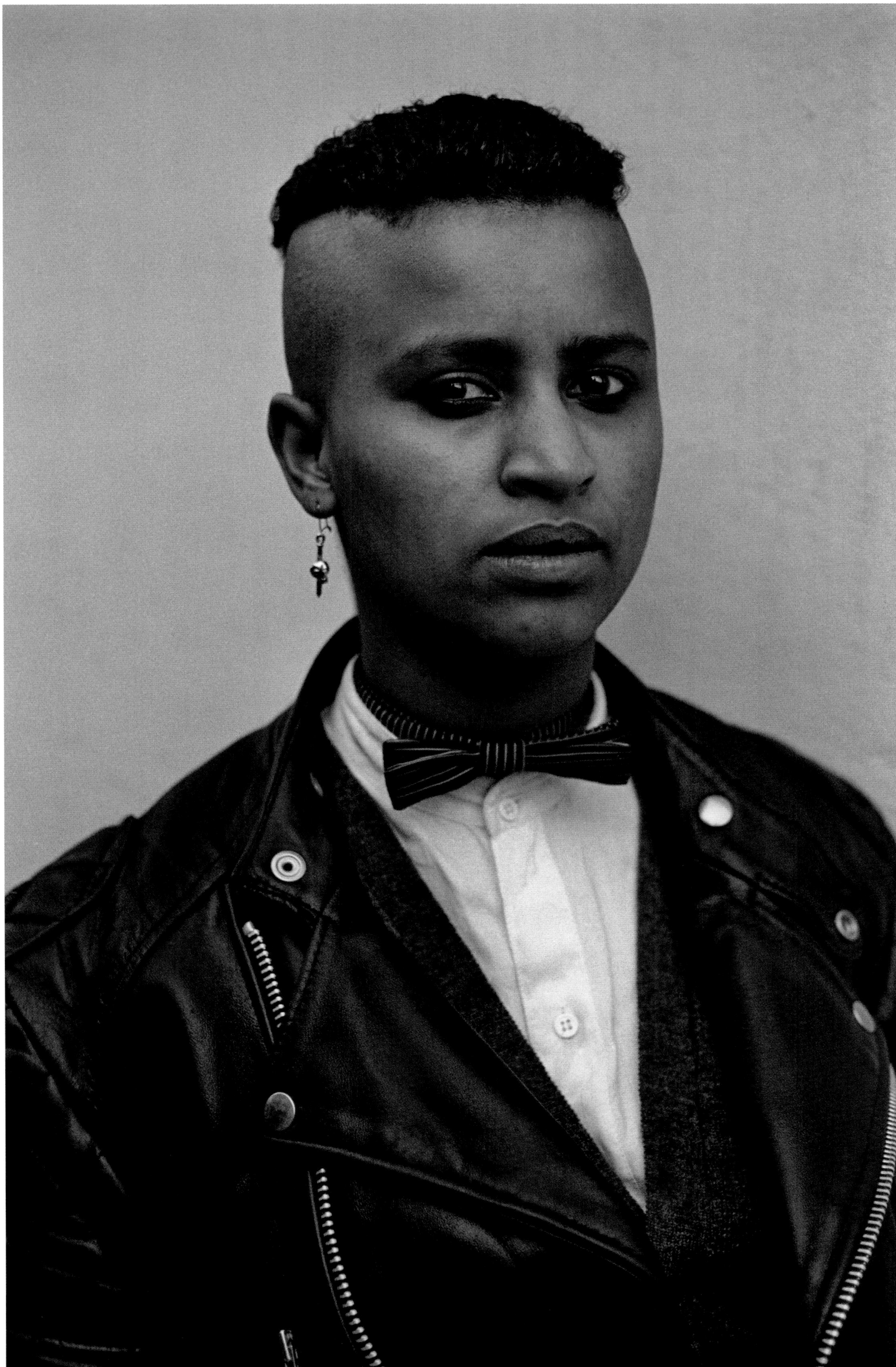

Hazel, Soho 1982.

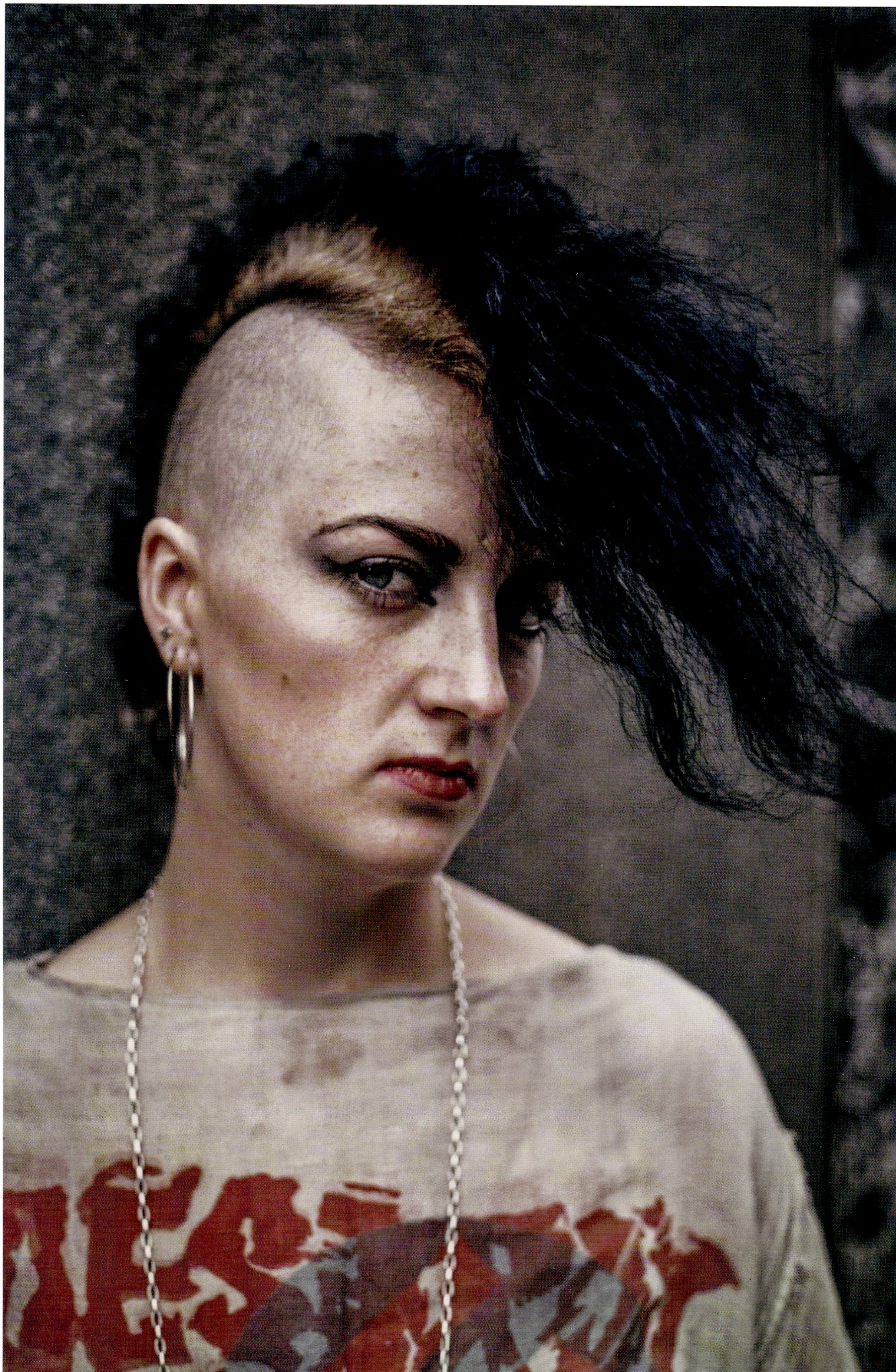

Julia, Le Beat Route, Soho 1981.

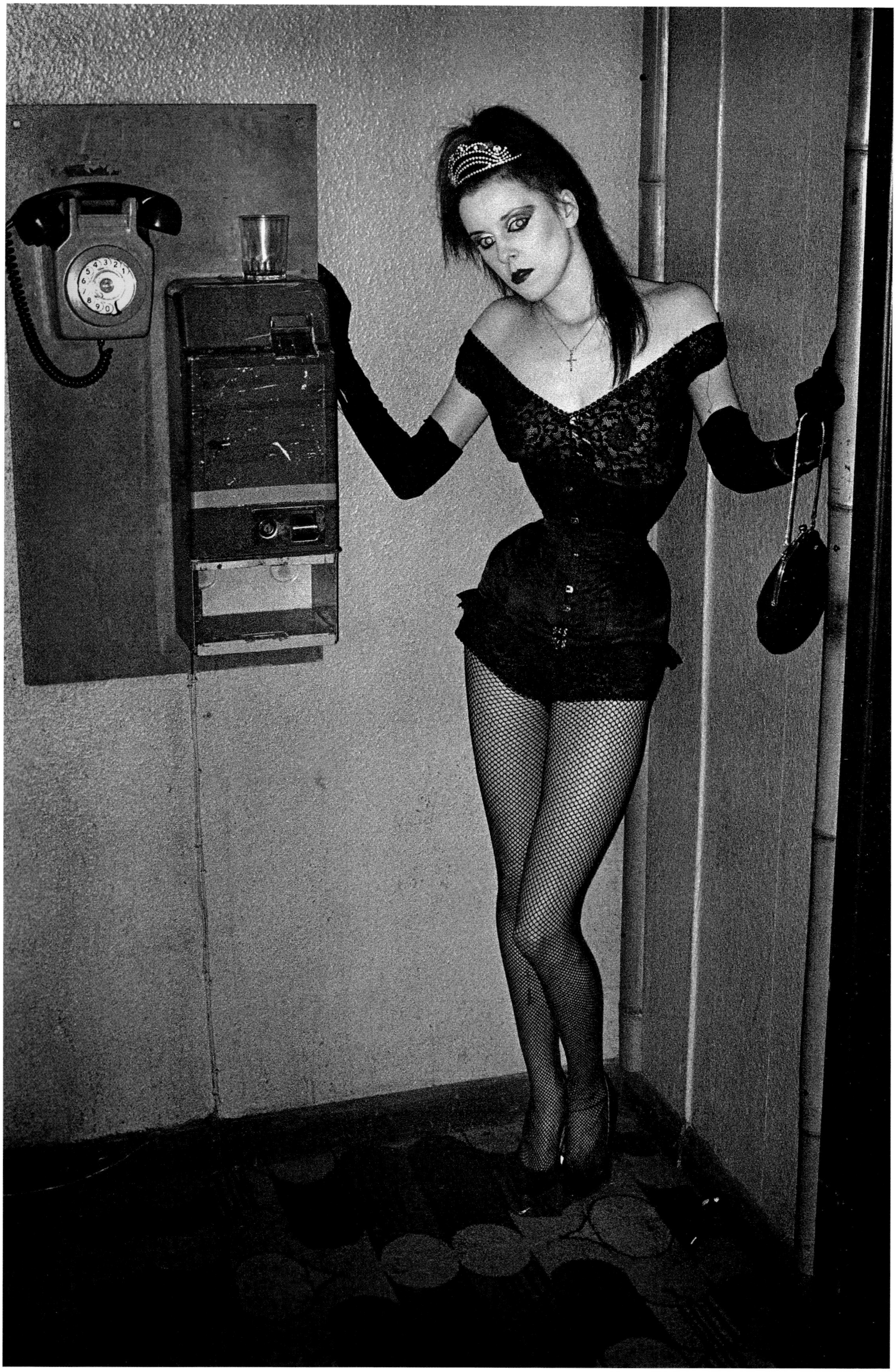

Helena, Chelsea 1982.

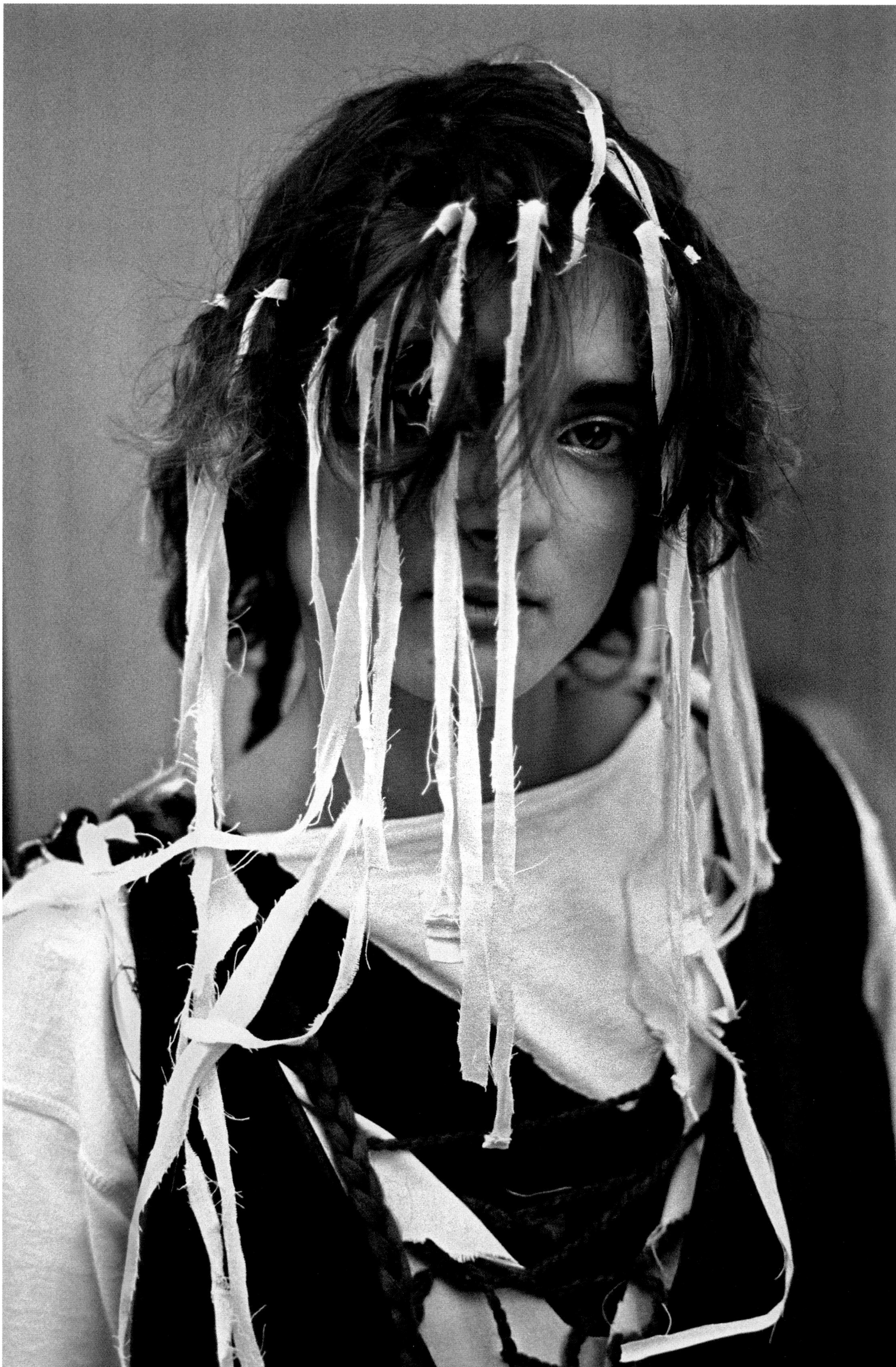

Charlotte, Notting Hill 1982.

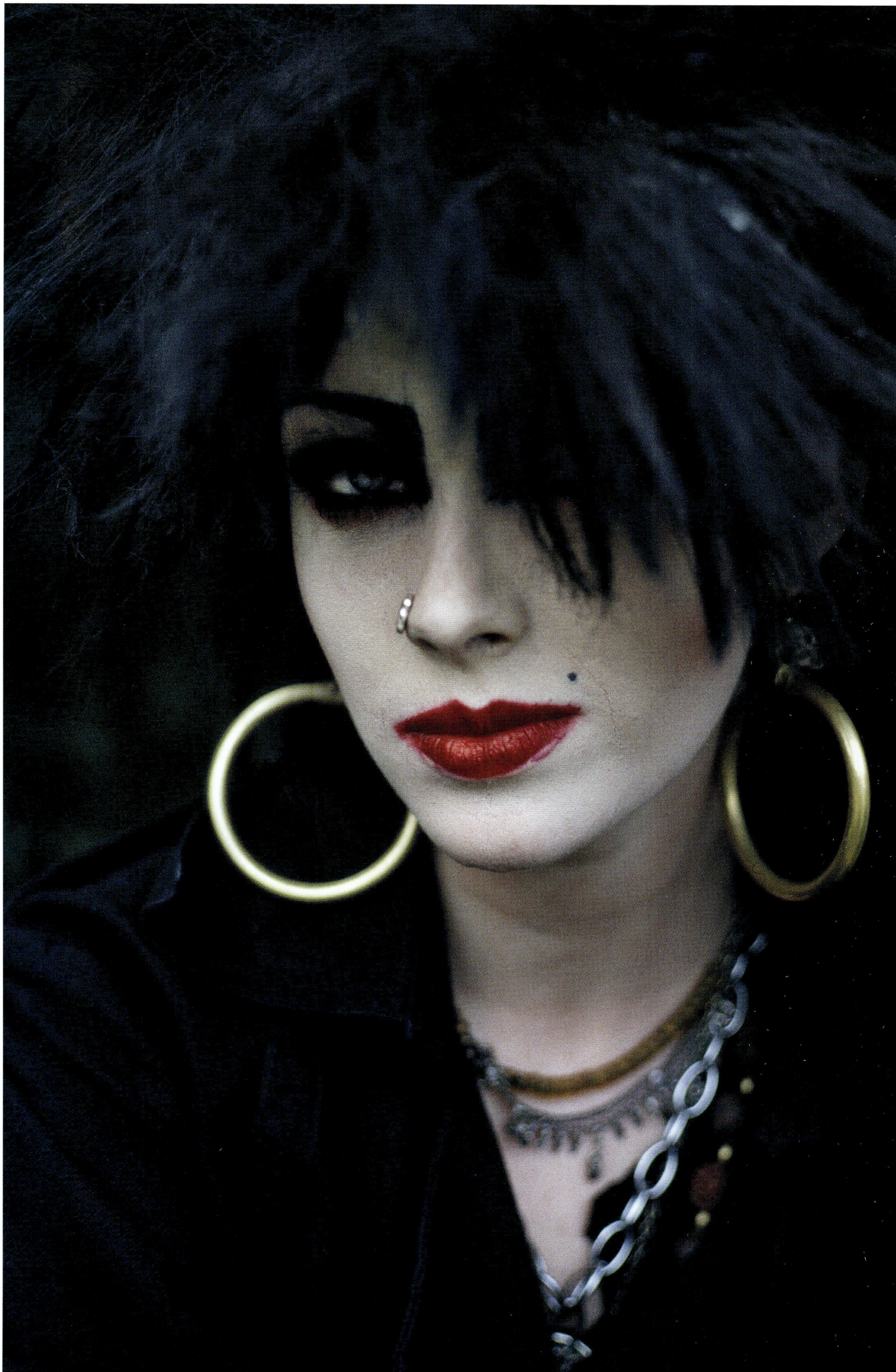

Crystalle, Skin Two, Soho 1983.

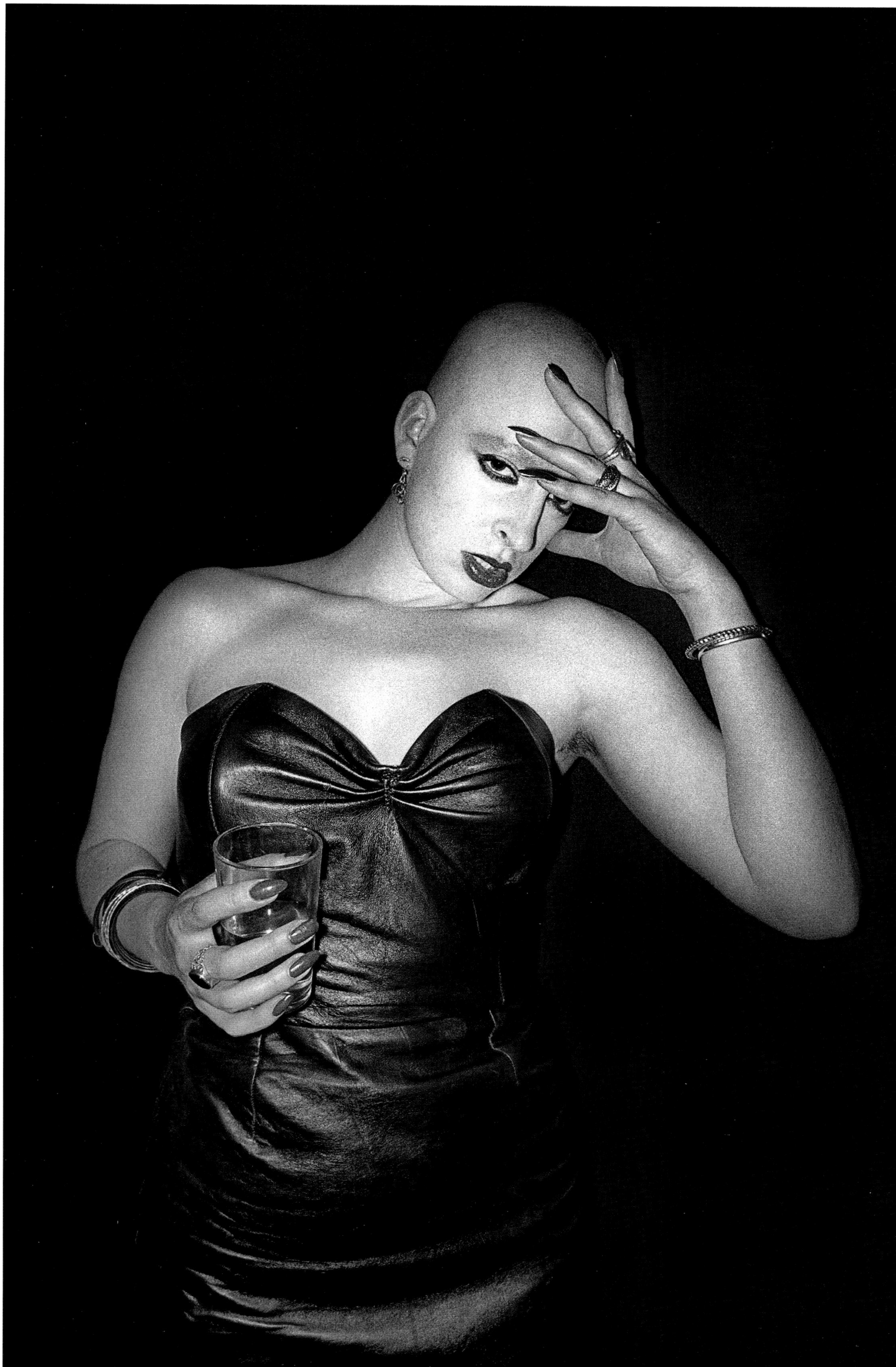

John, Camden Palace 1982.

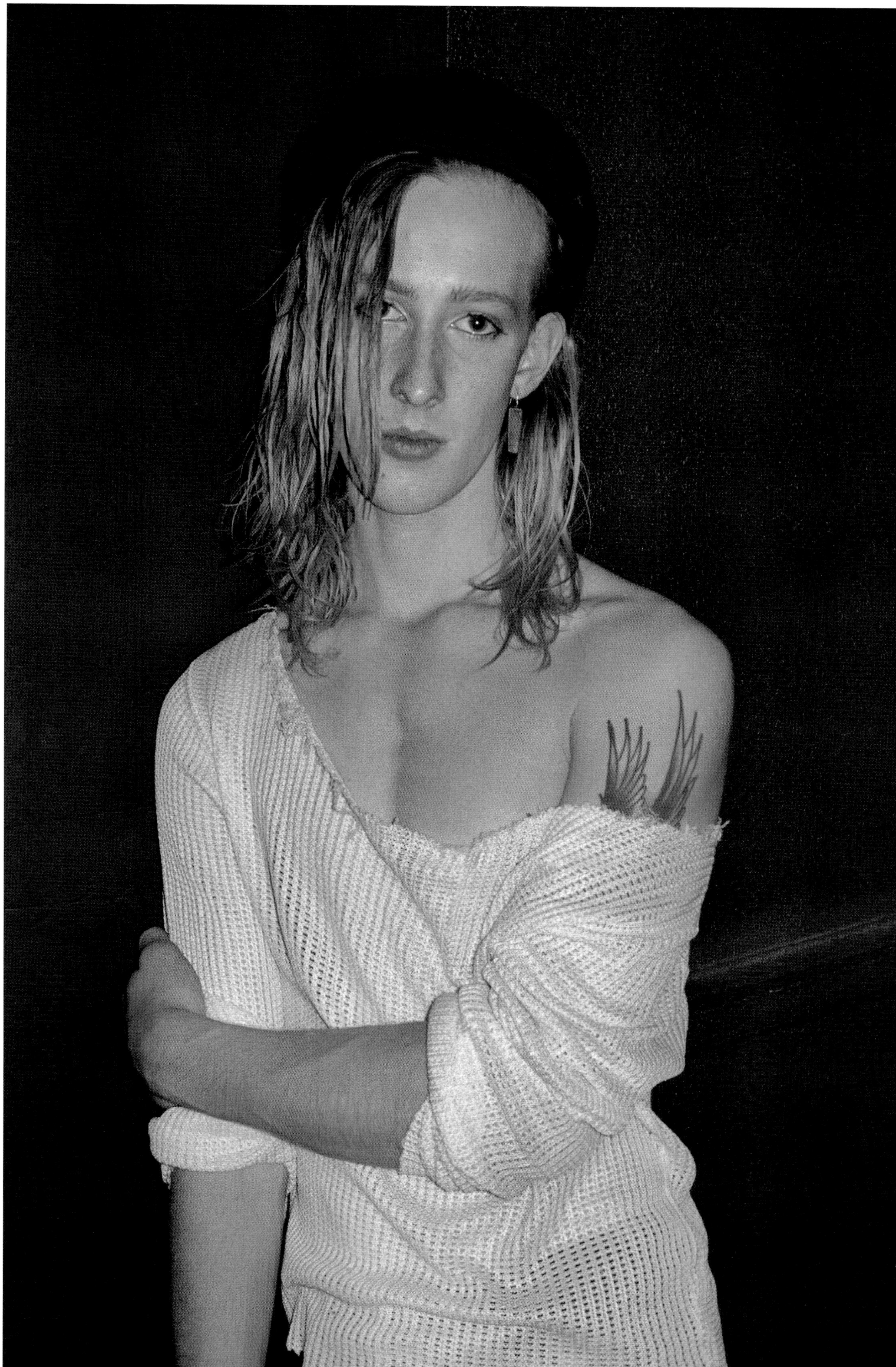

Gabrielle, King's Road, Chelsea 1982.

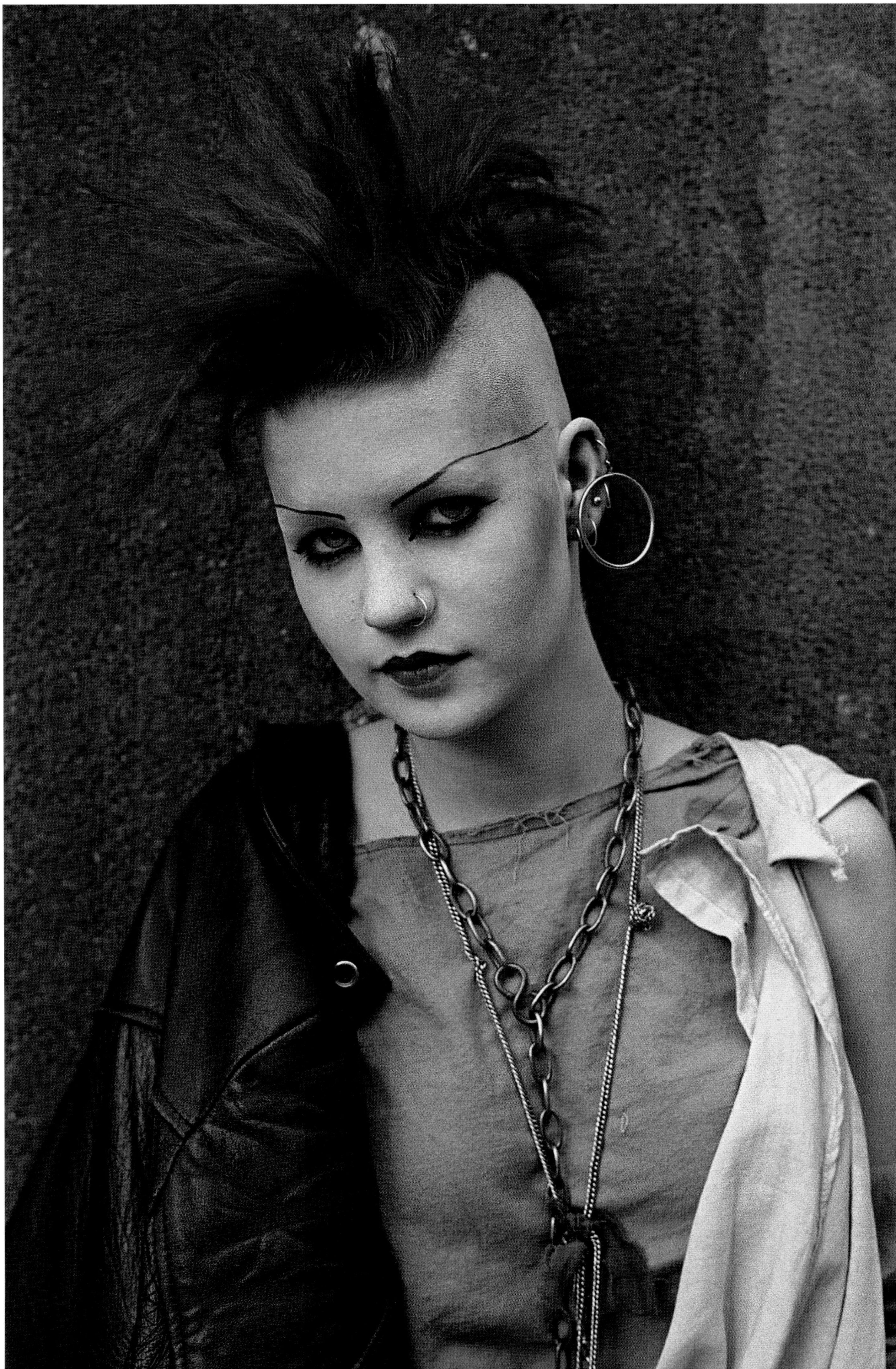

Pim, Skin Two, Soho 1983.

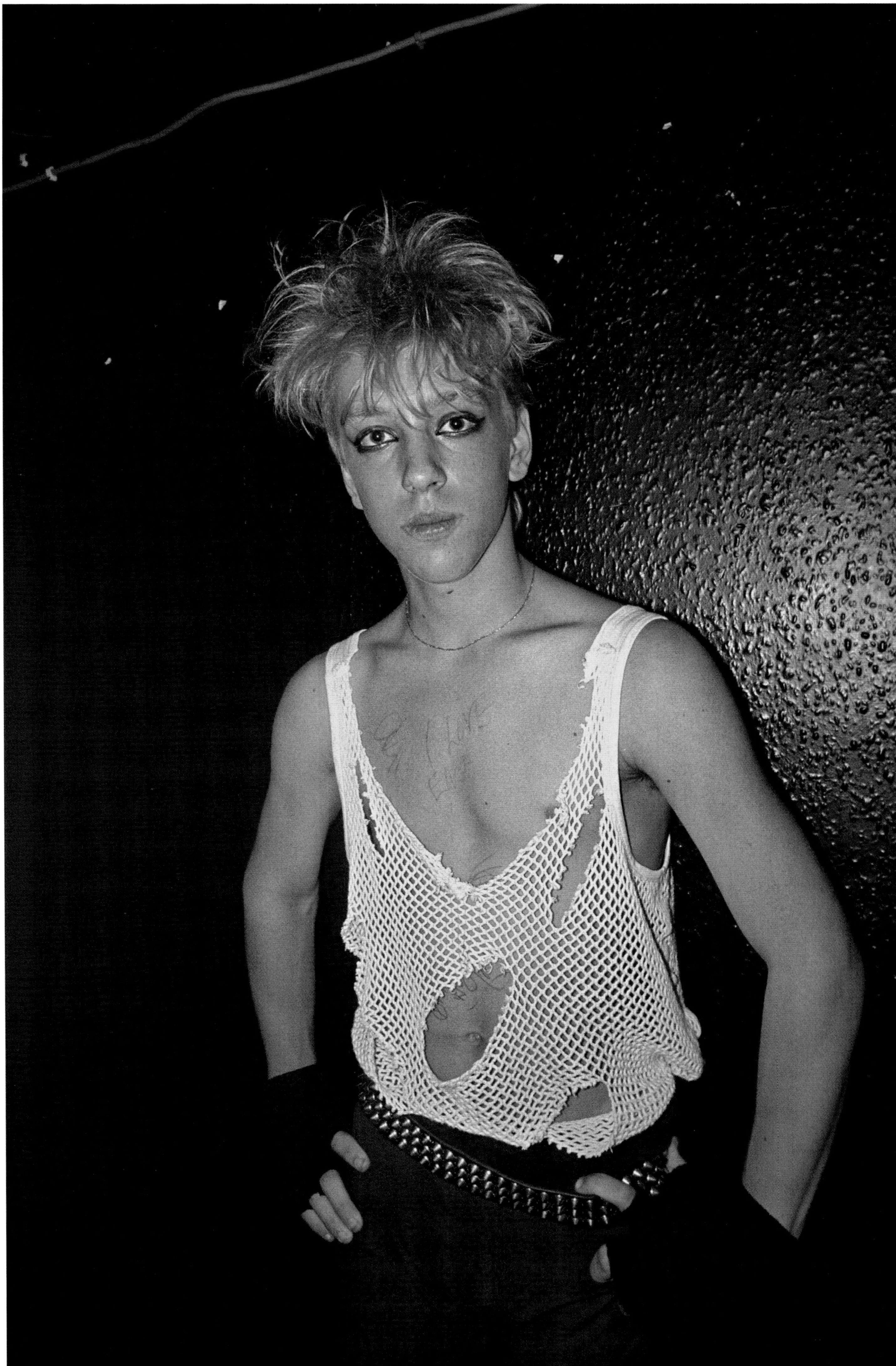

Tracey, The Batcave, Soho 1982.

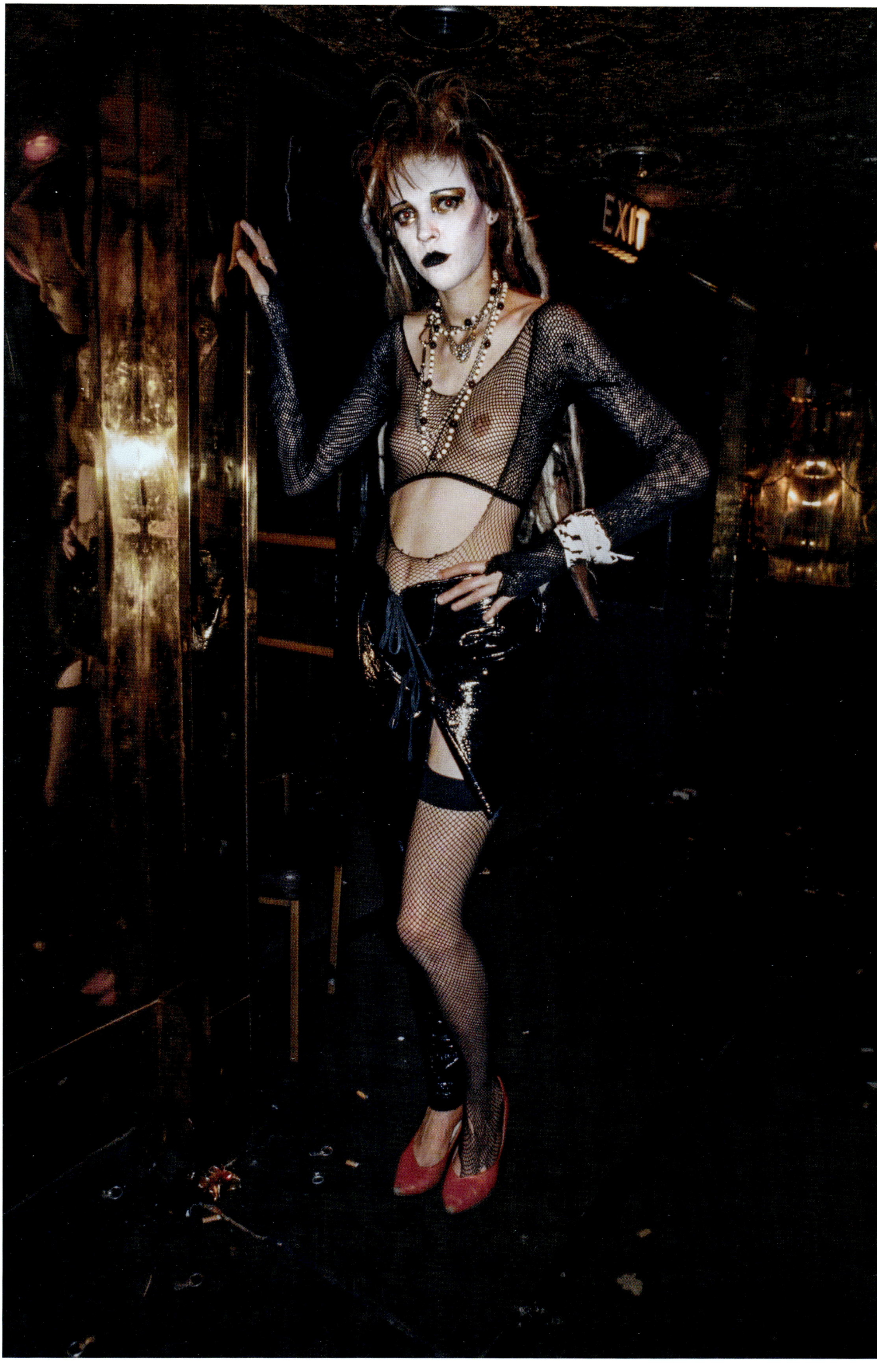
EXIT

Name unknown, Mud Club, Soho 1984.

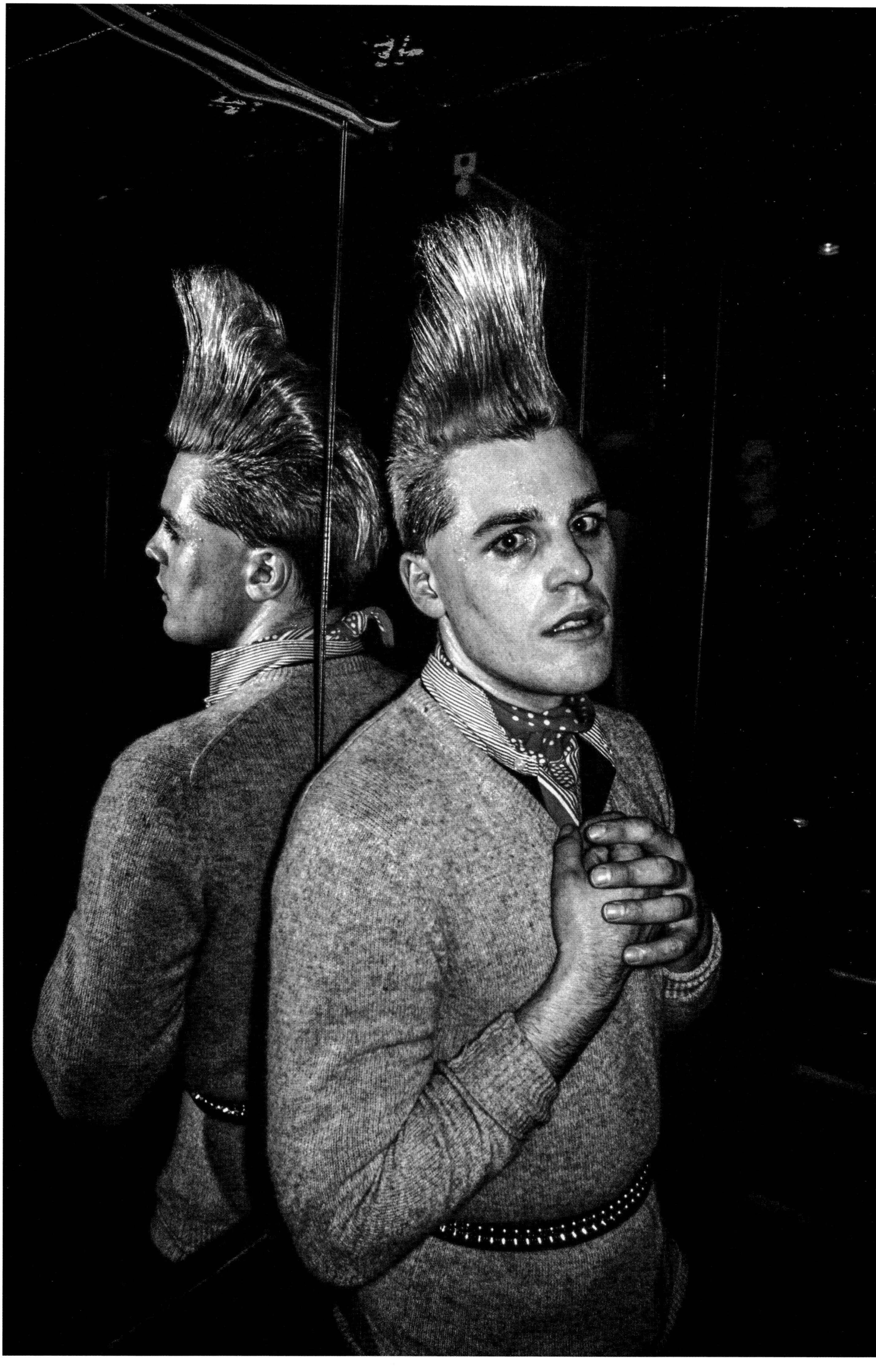

Myra, Le Beat Route, Soho 1981.

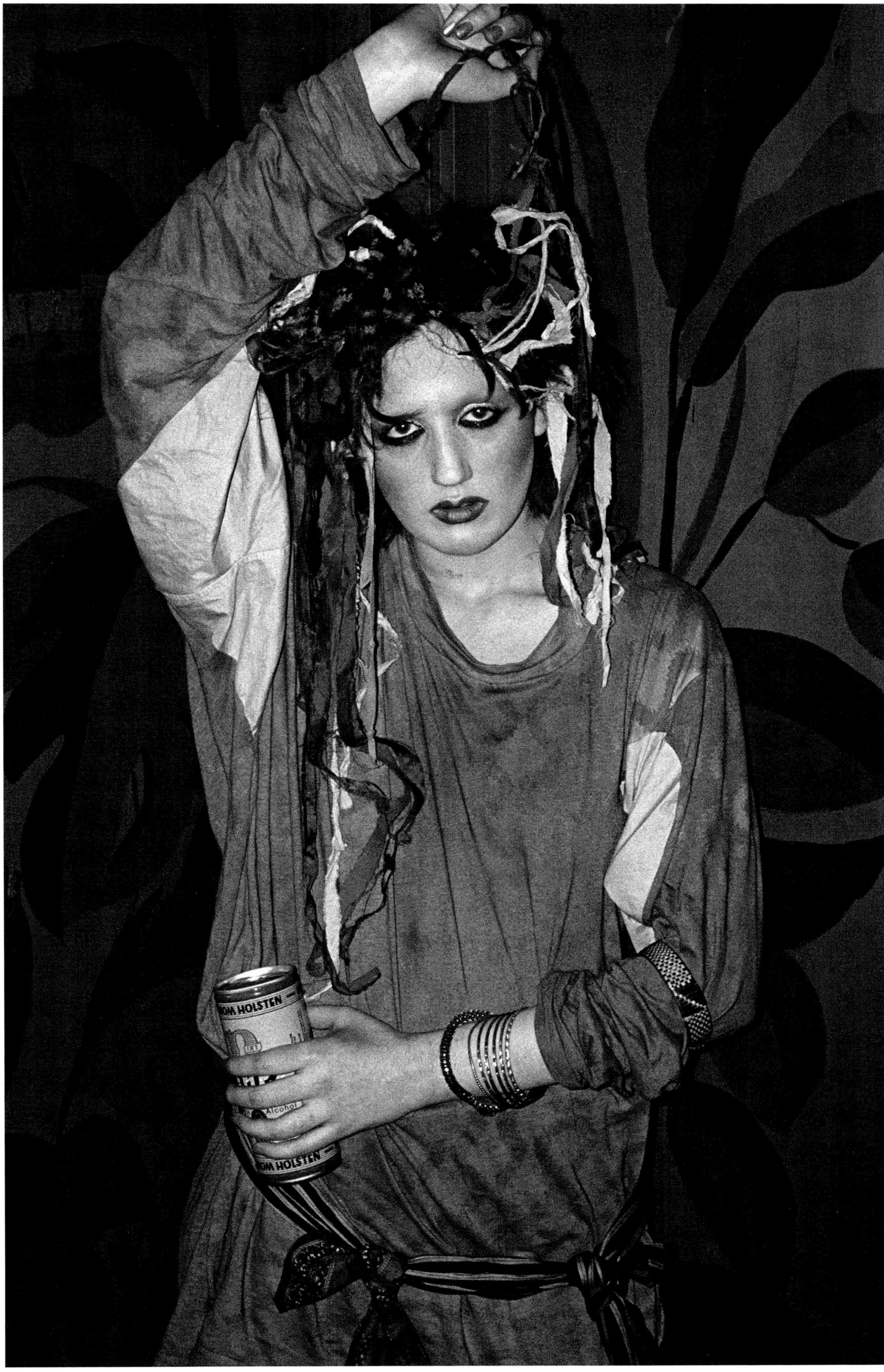
OM HOLSTEN
Alcohol
OM HOLSTEN

Name unknown, Soho 1984.

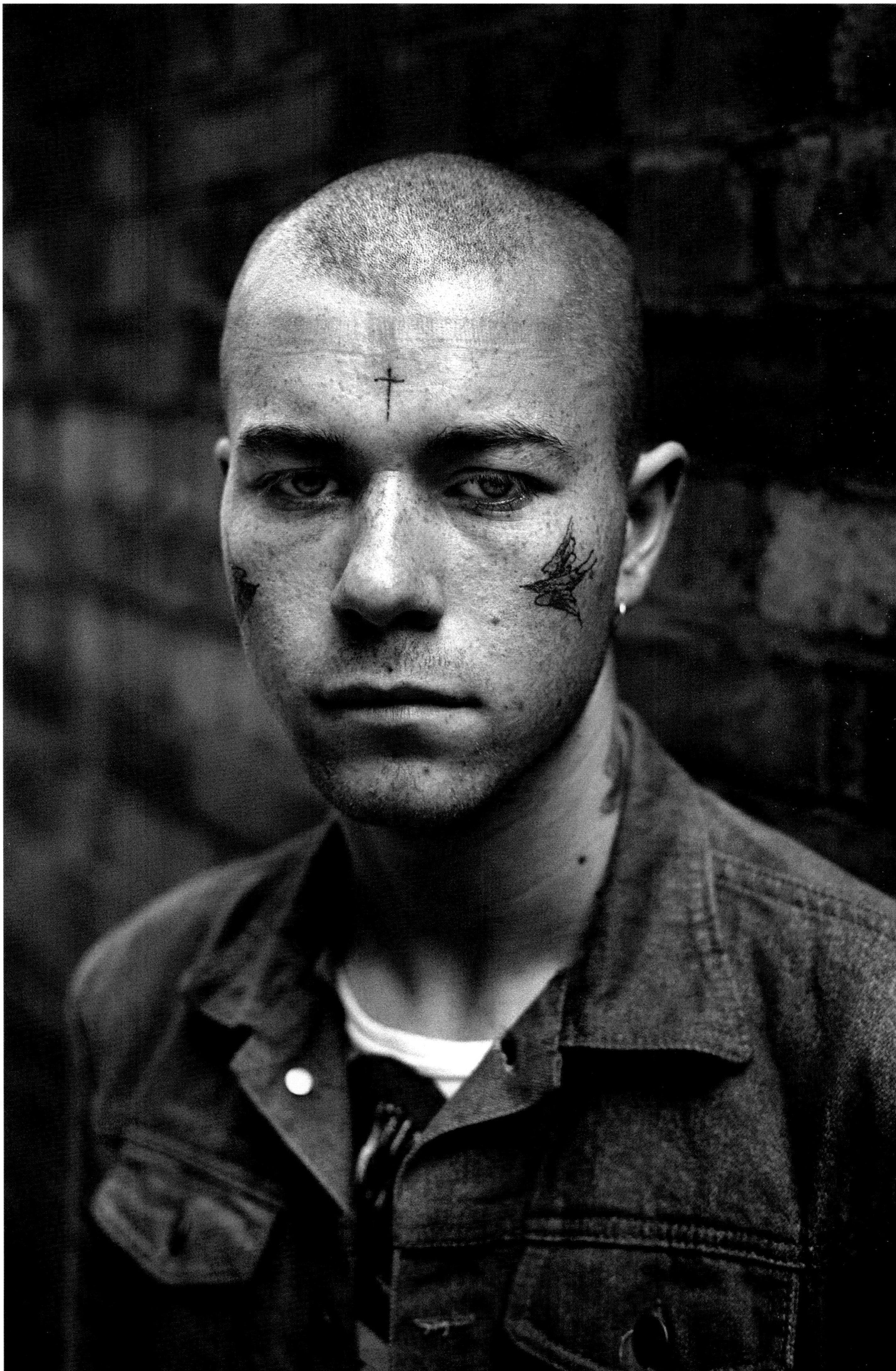

Donna, Leicester Square 1982.

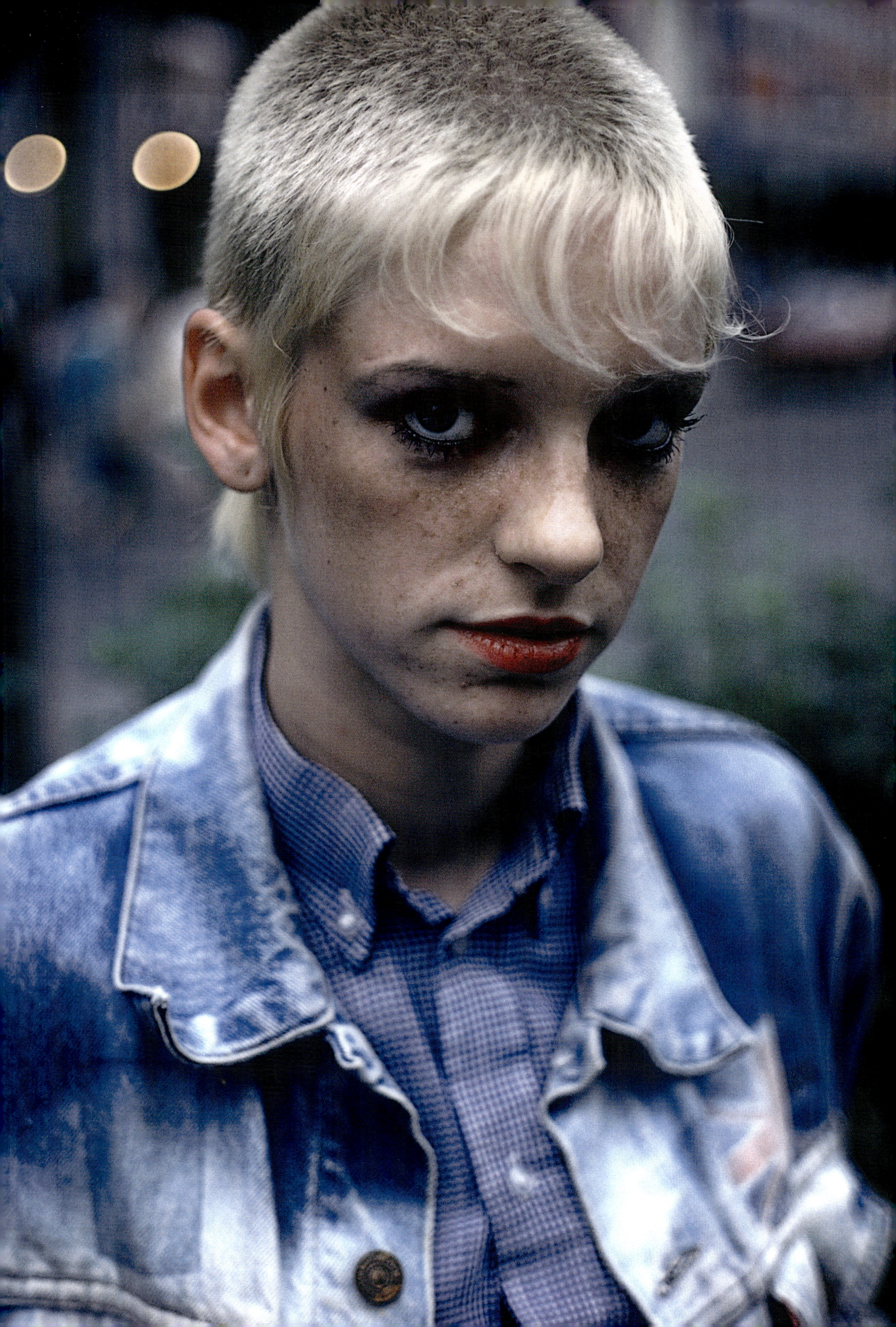

Shelley, Brixton 1984.

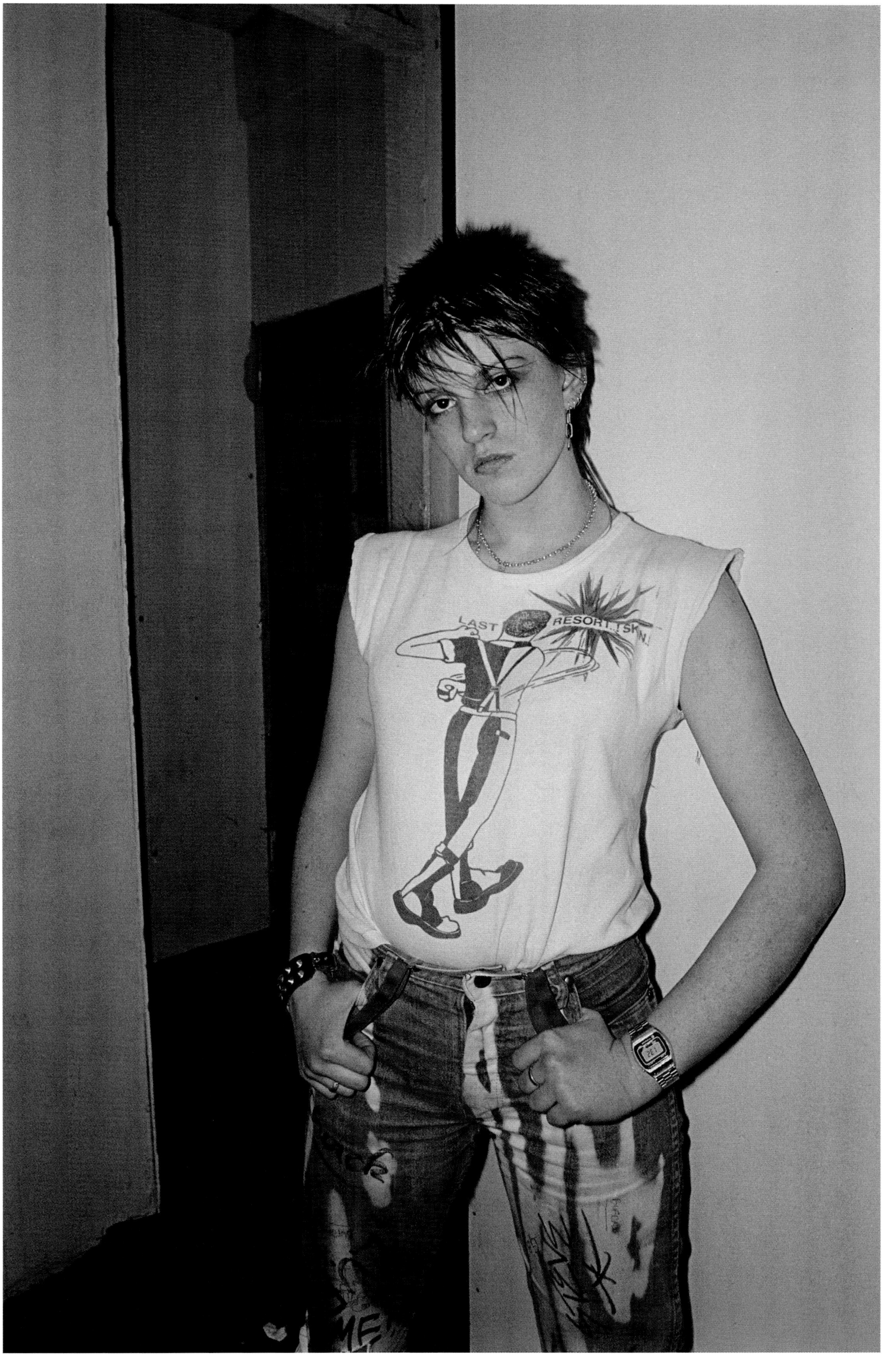
LAST RESORT

Patti, Camden Palace 1983.

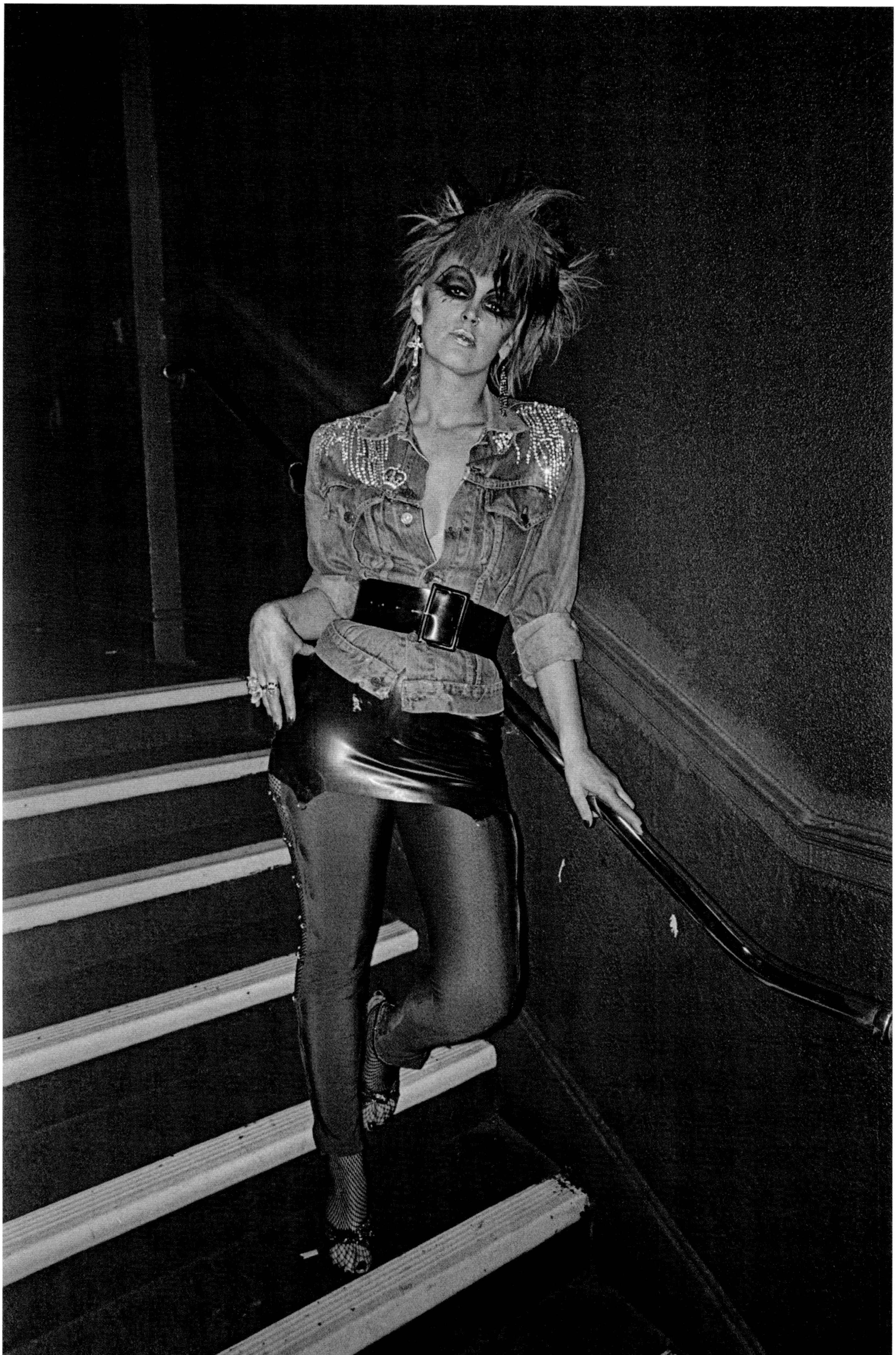

Gary, Leicester Square 1982.

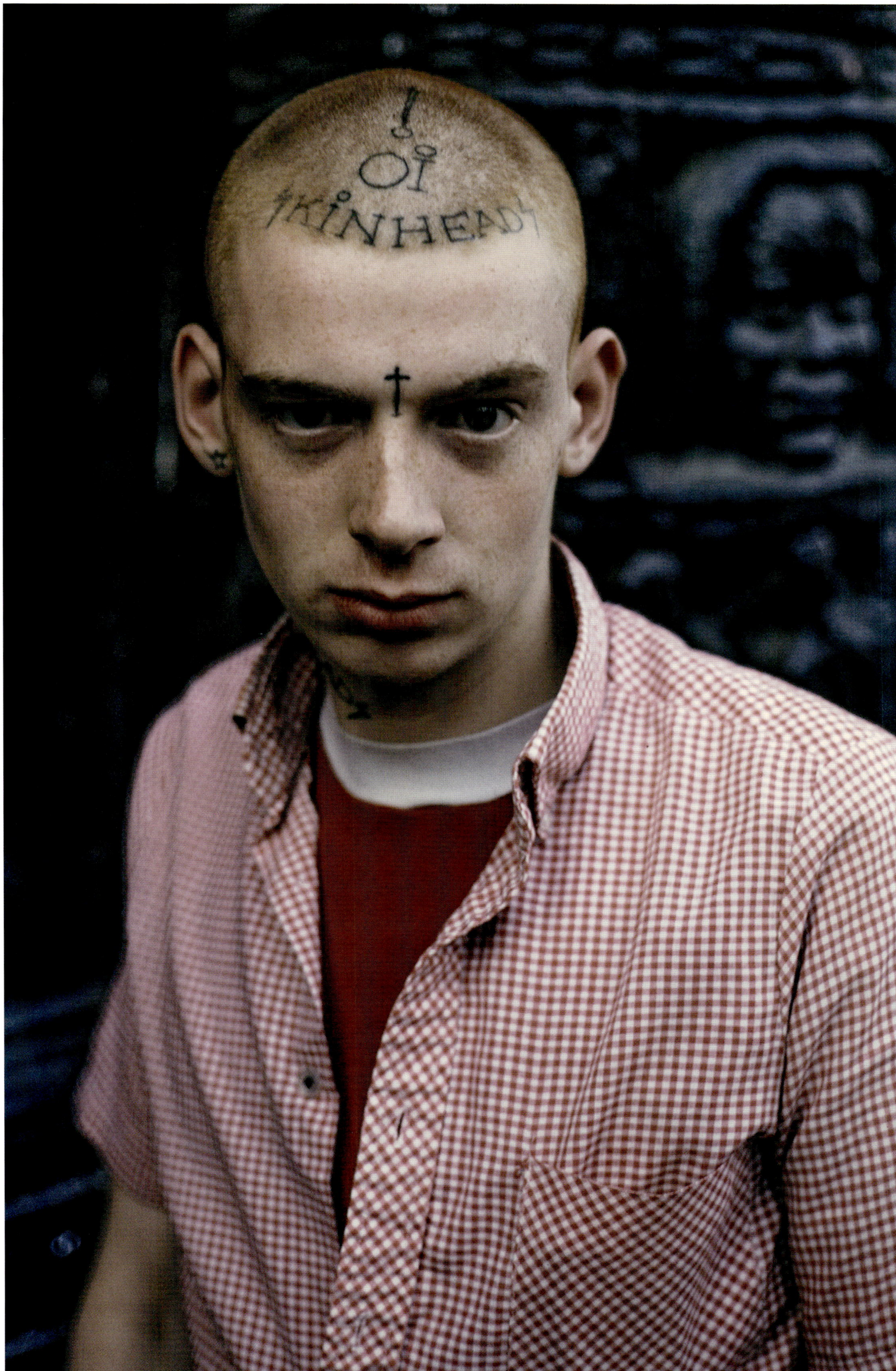

Elizabeth, Le Beat Route 1982.

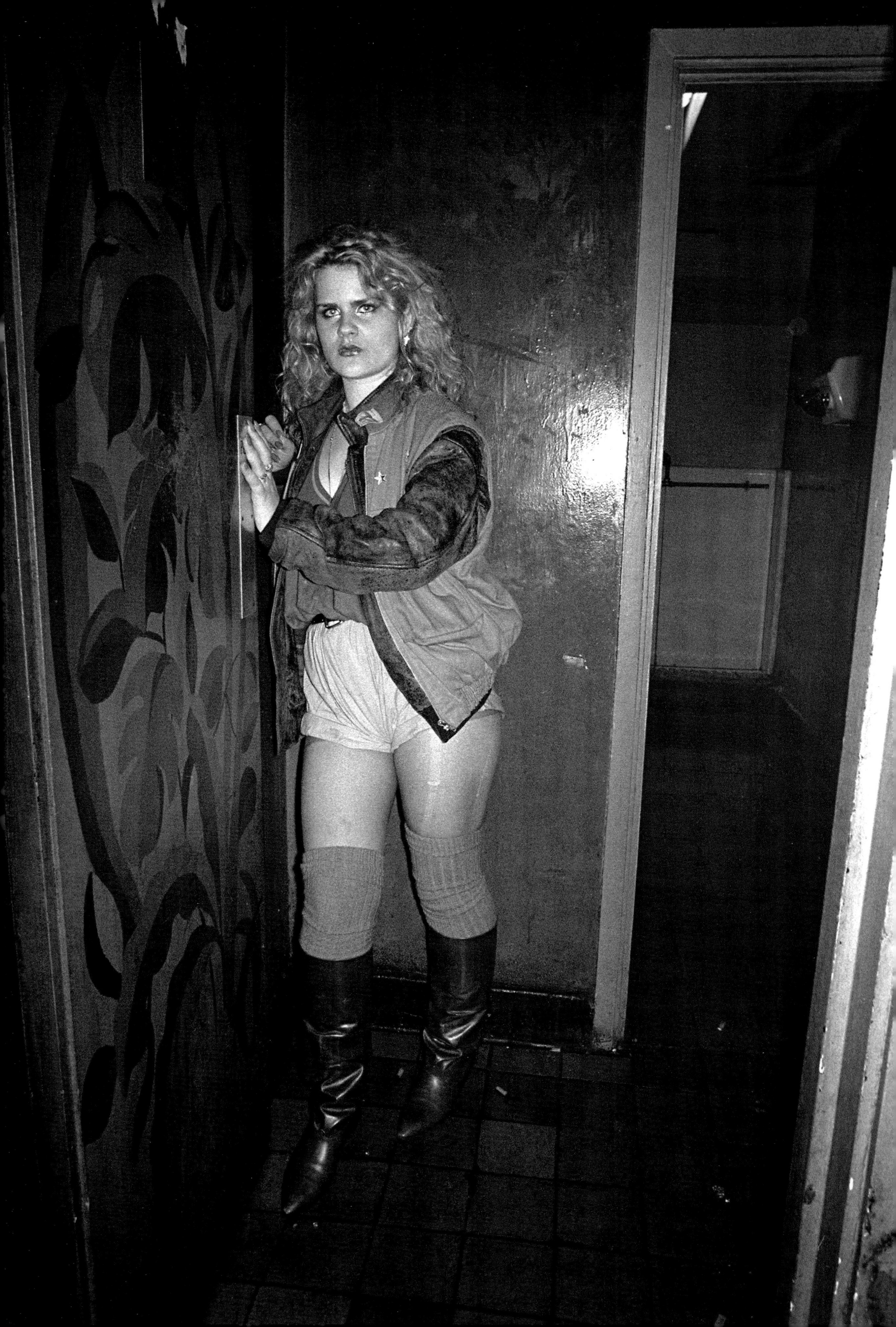

Jane, Skin Two, Soho 1983.

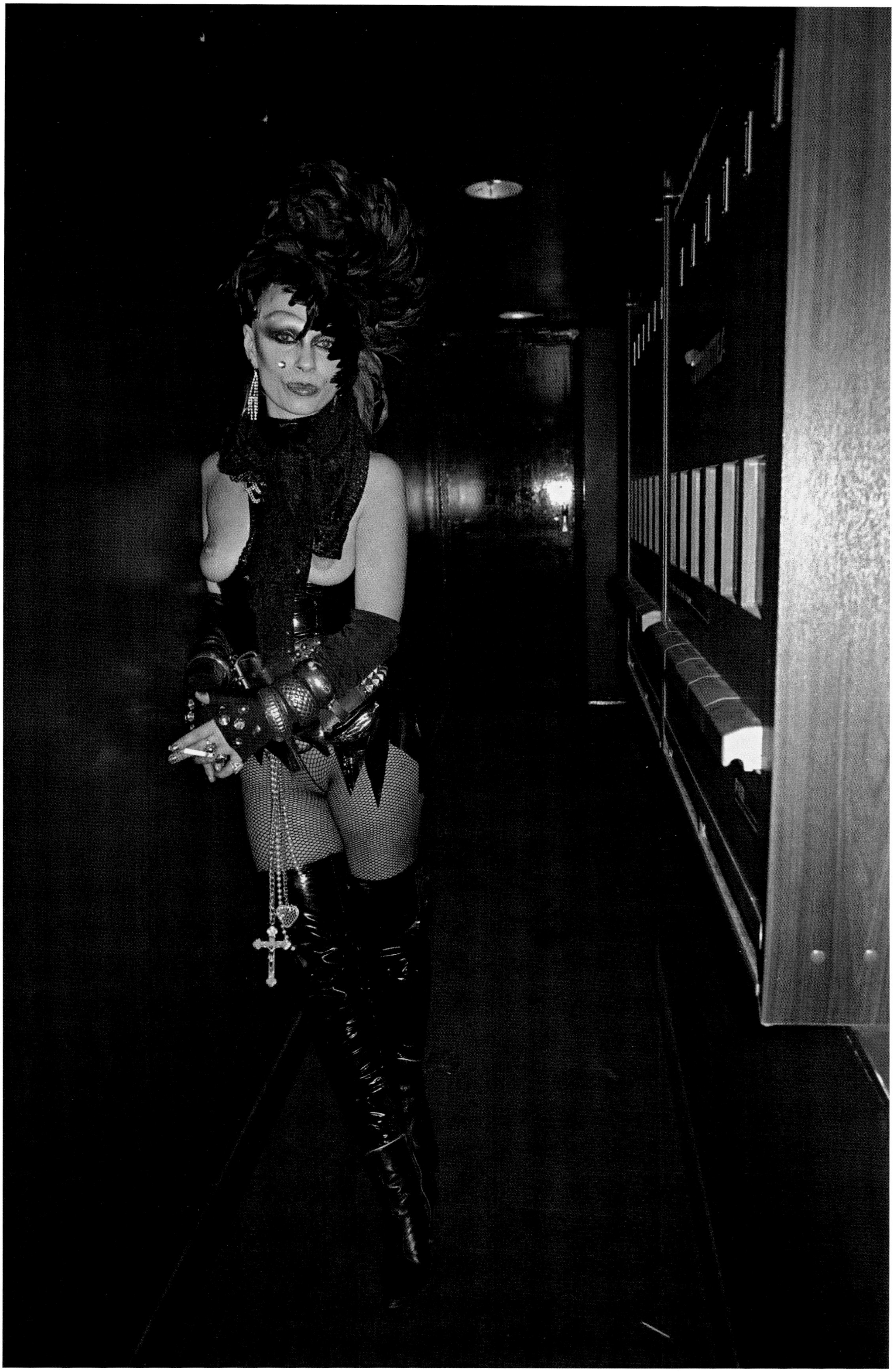

Chris aka Scar, Goulston Street, Aldgate 1981.

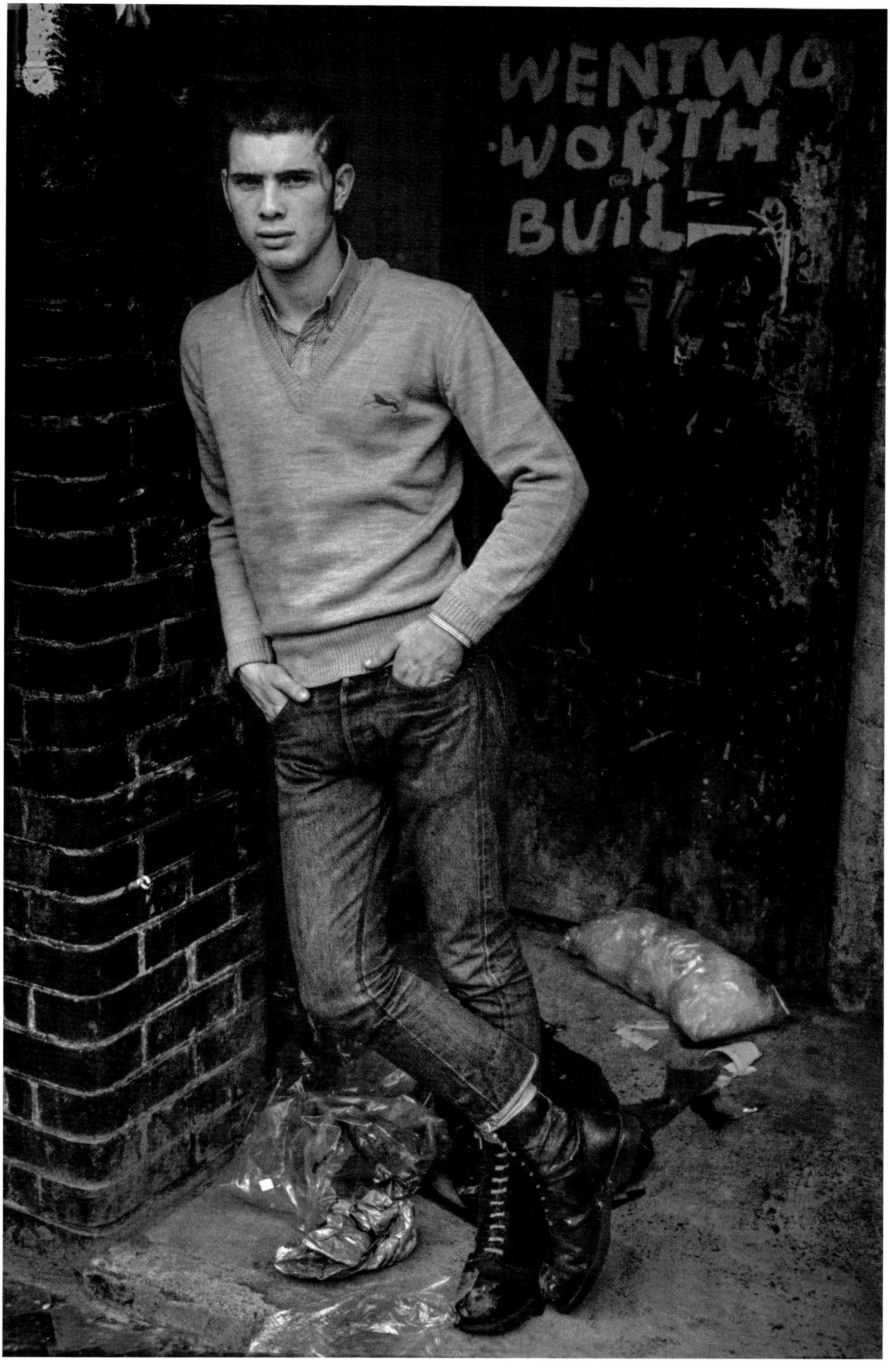
WENTWO
WORTH
BUIL

Paul, Leicester Square 1981.

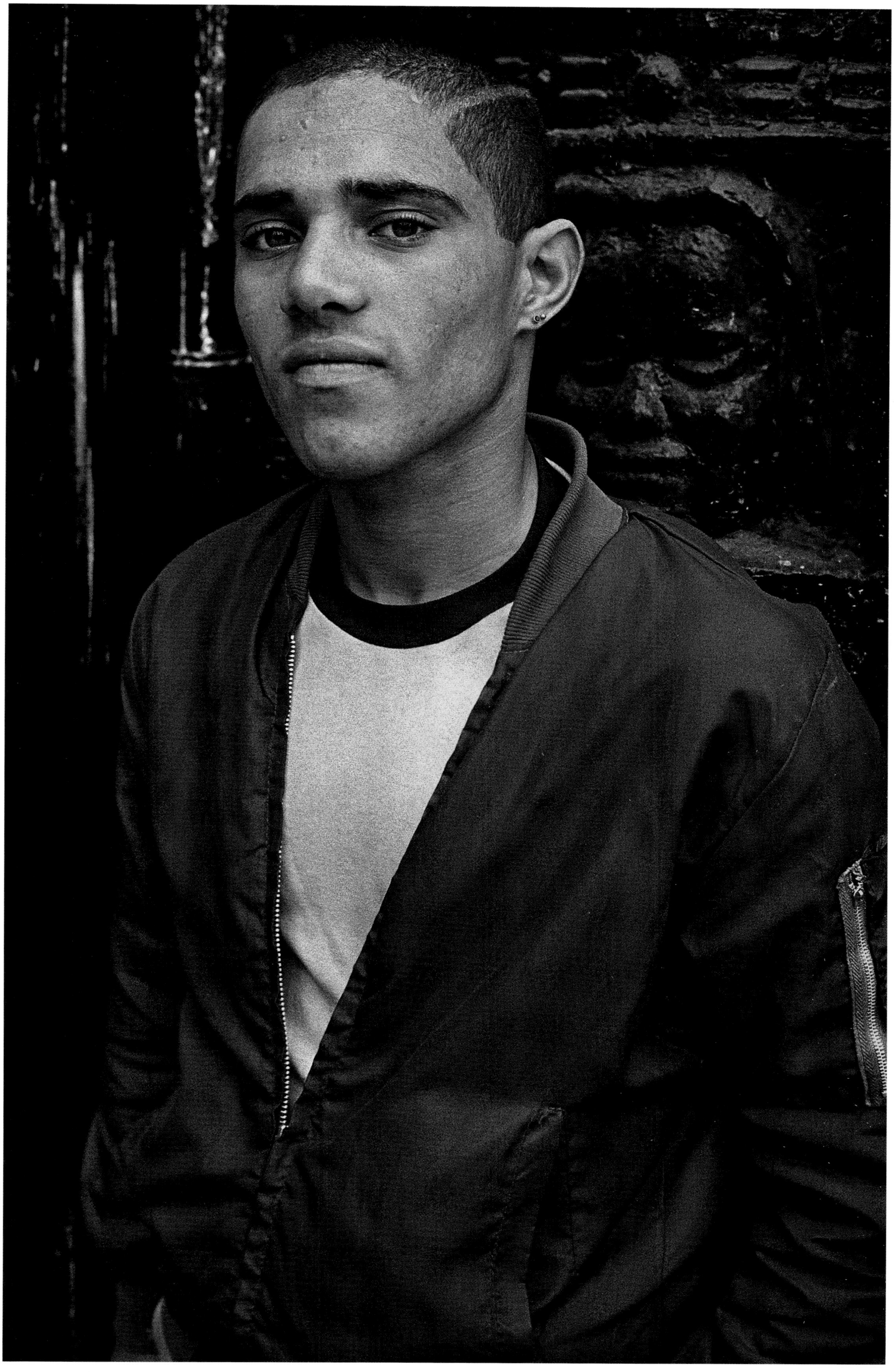

Name unknown, Brixton 1984.

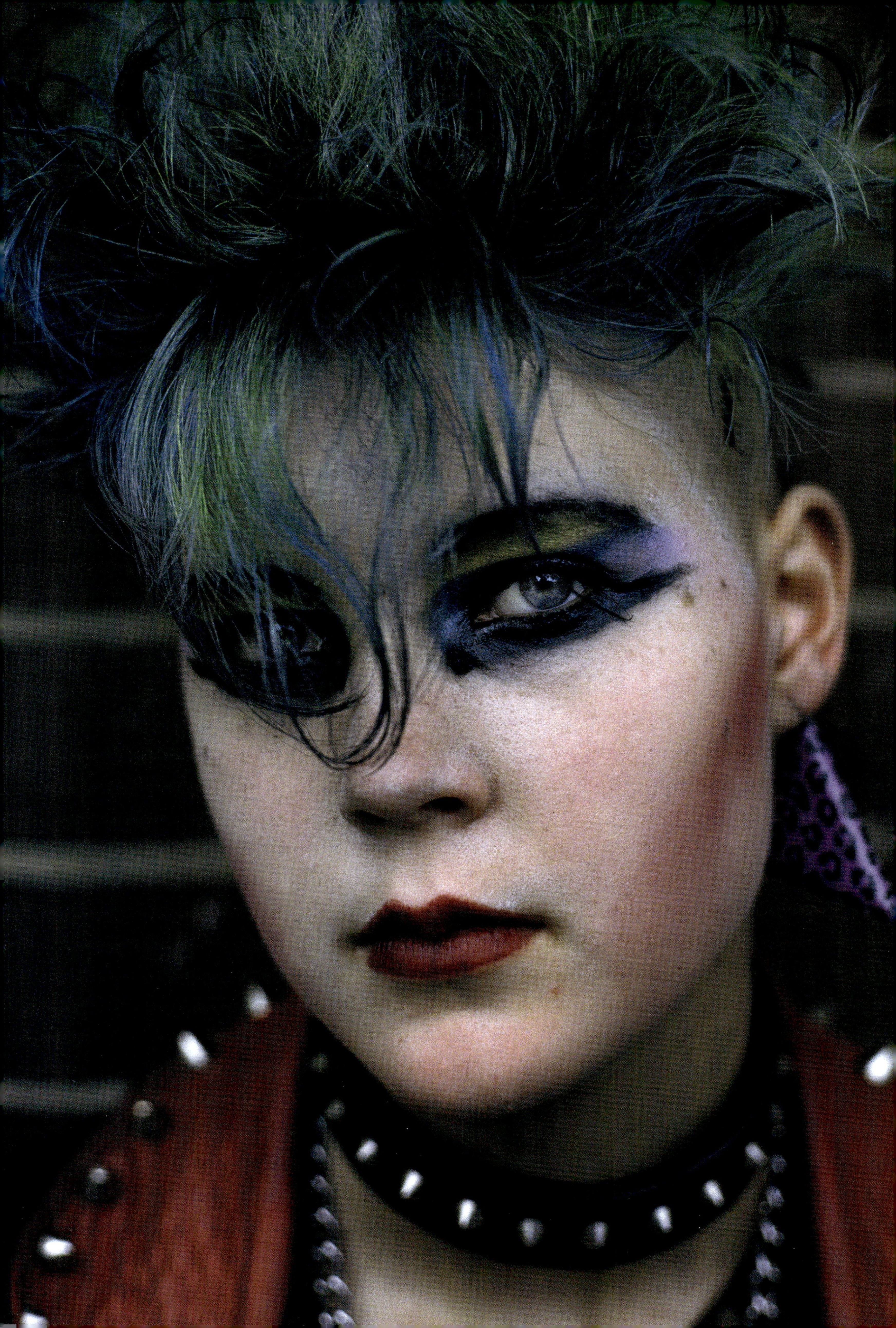

Sarah, Tribe club, Leicester Square 1986.

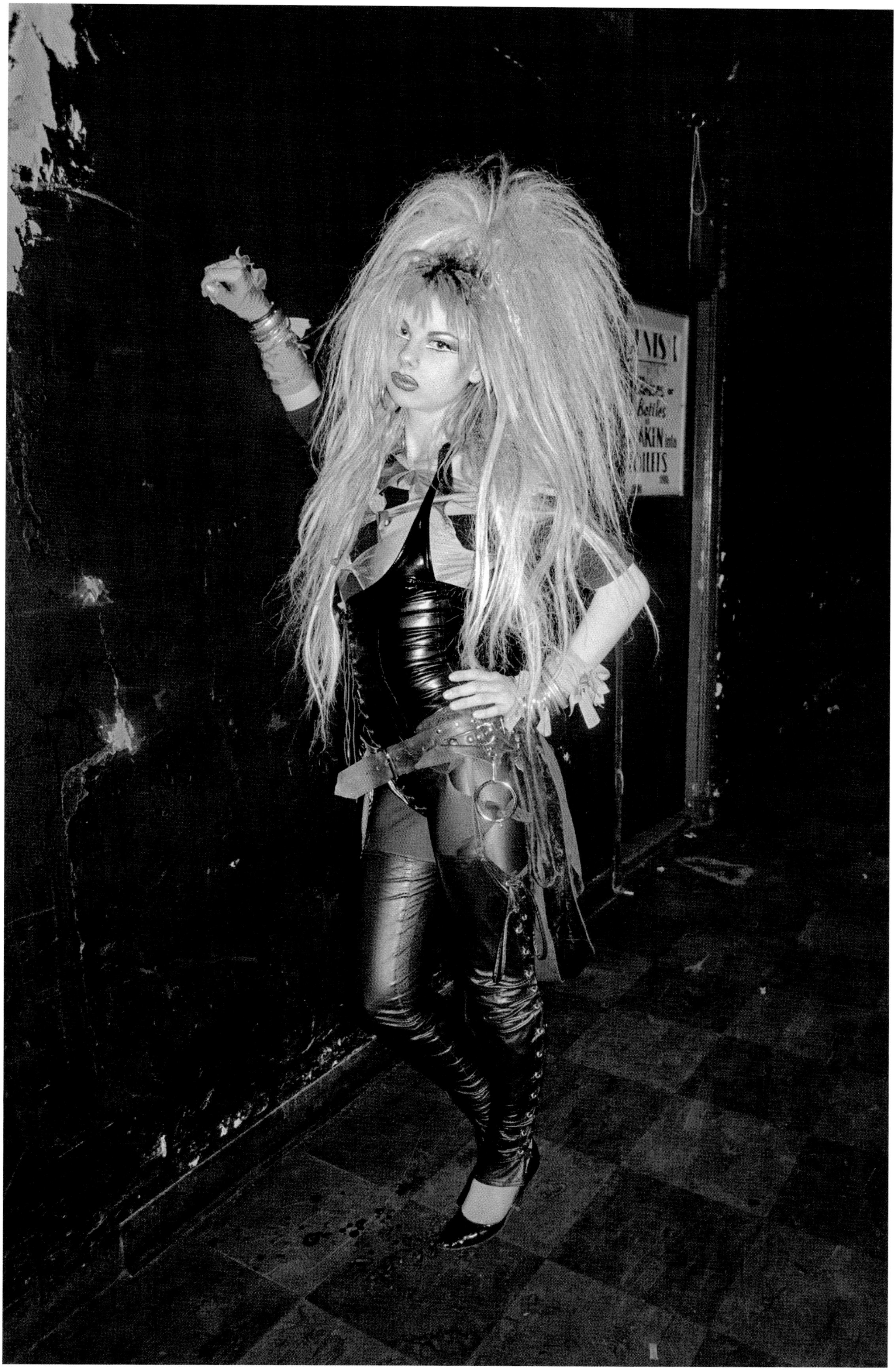
Bottles
into

Mark, Chelsea 1983.

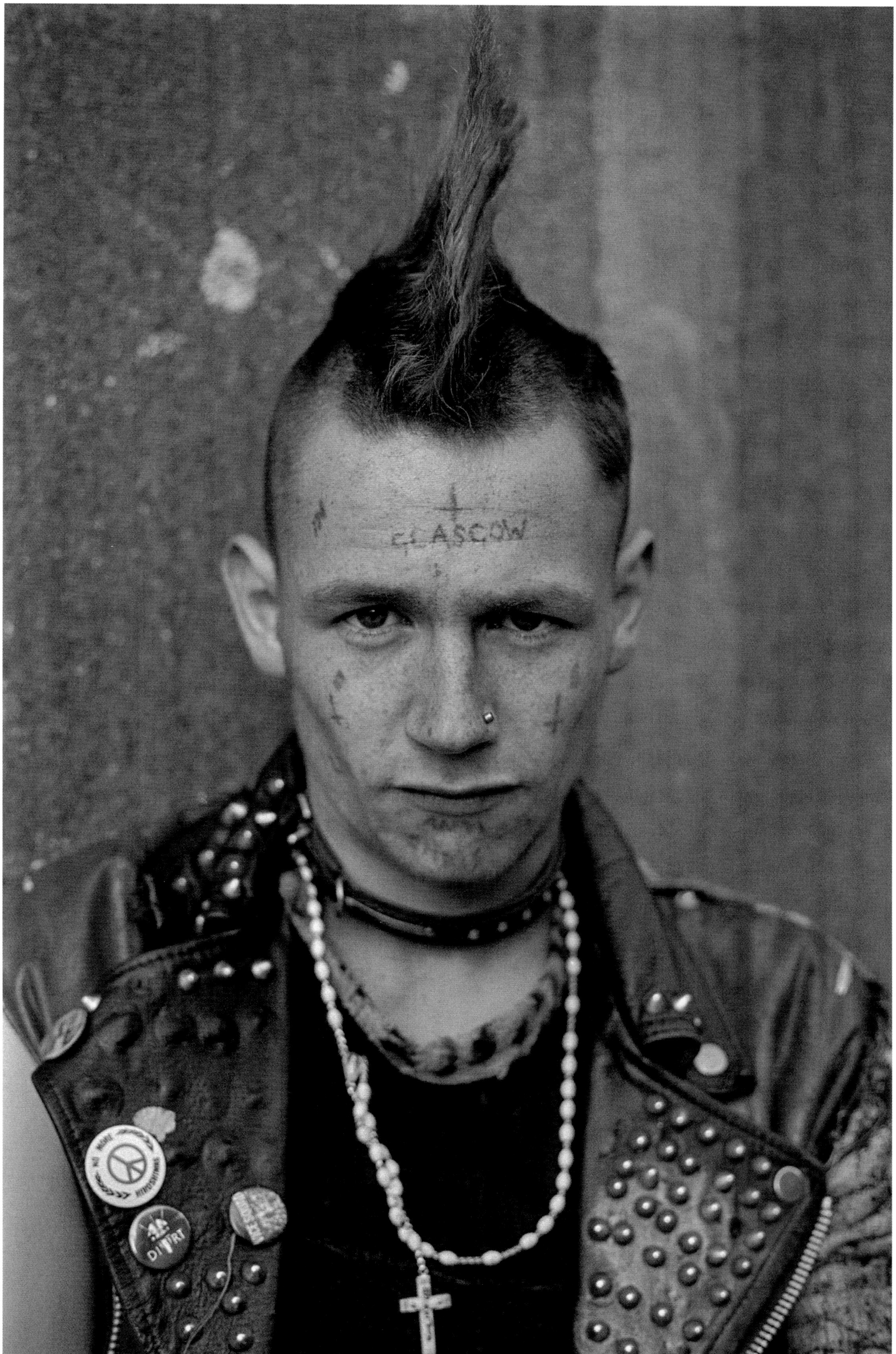

Malcolm, King's Road, Chelsea 1983.

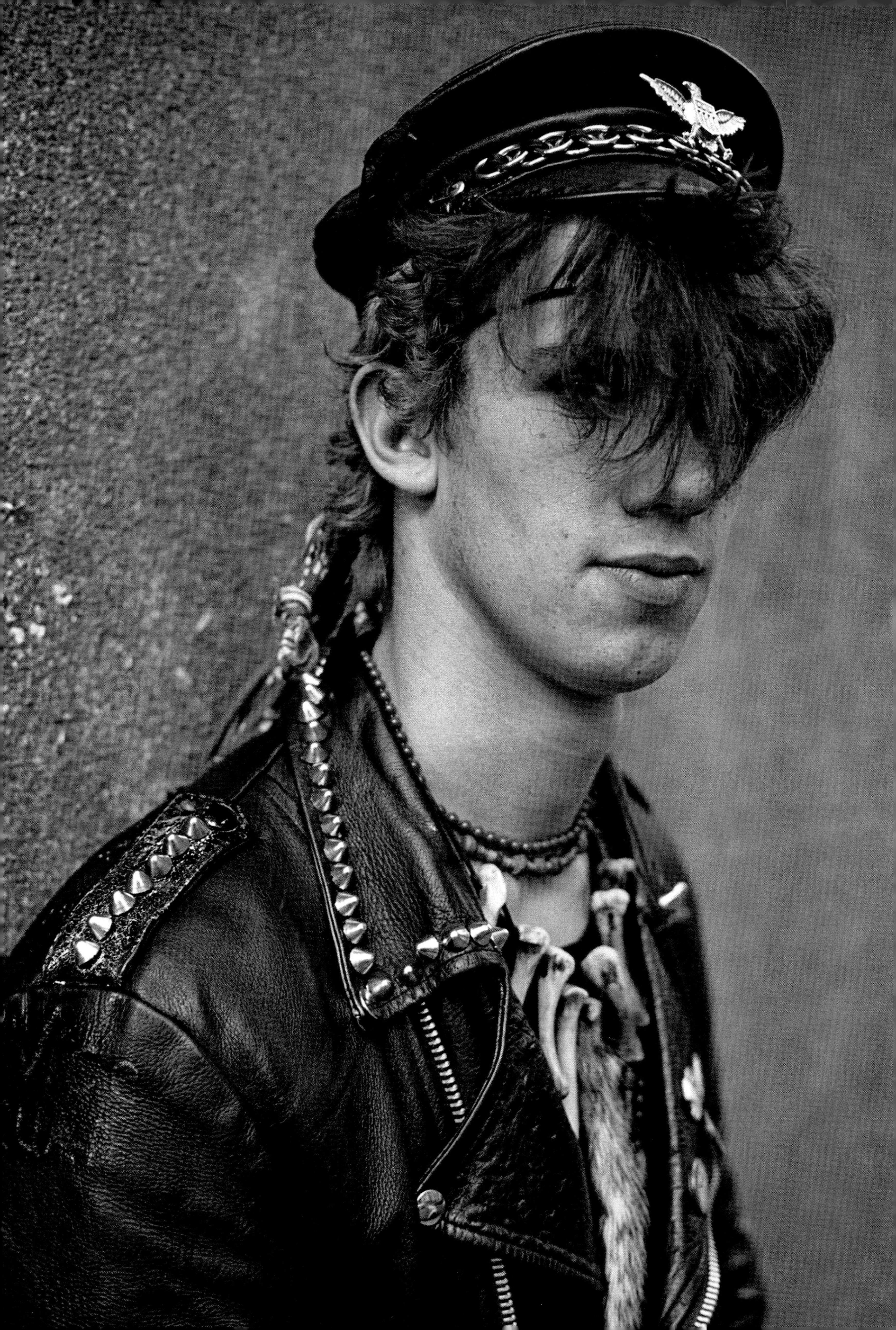

Yar, King's Road 1983.

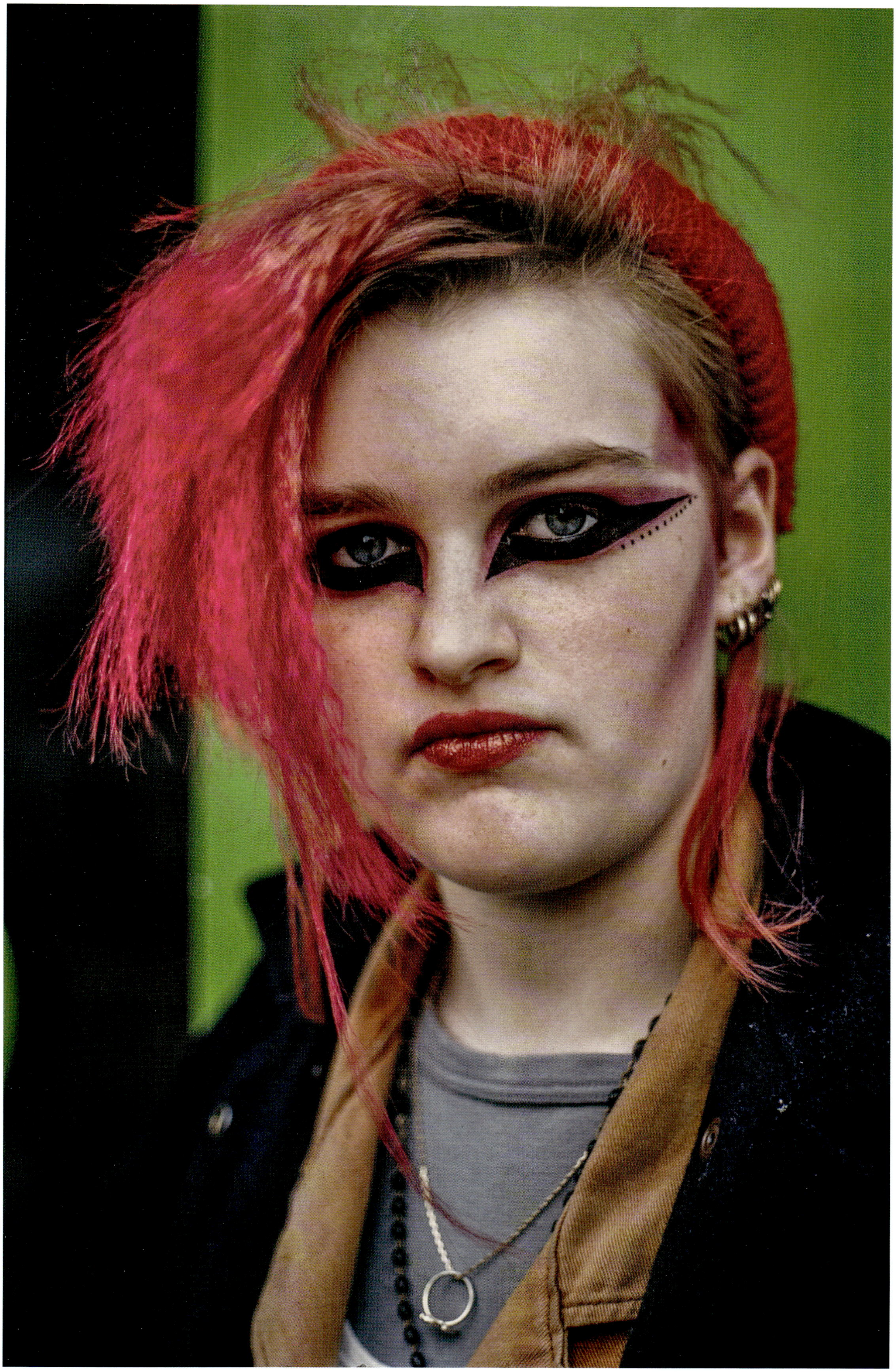

Steve, Soho 1988.

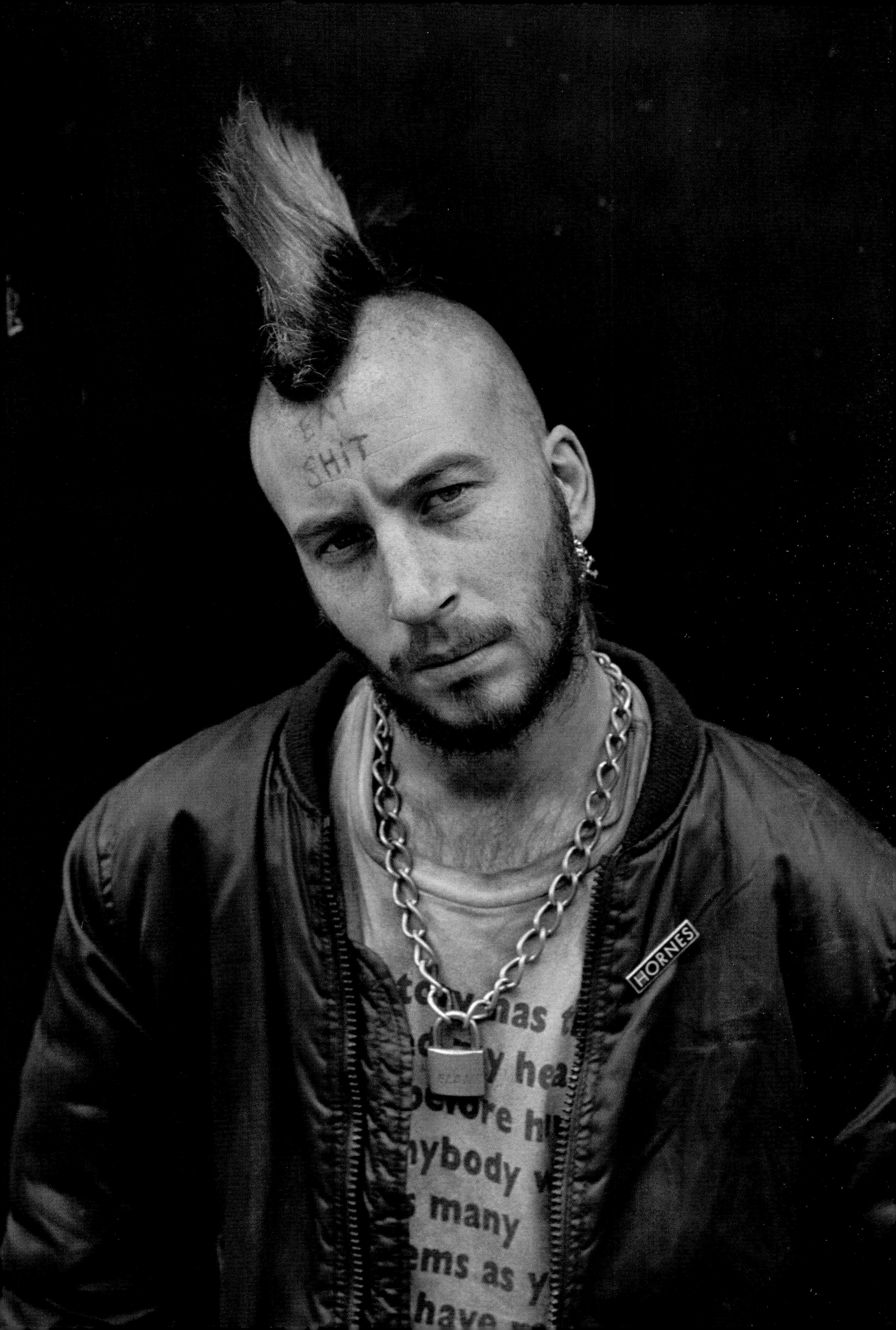
SHIT
HORNES

Jane, Camden Palace 1982.

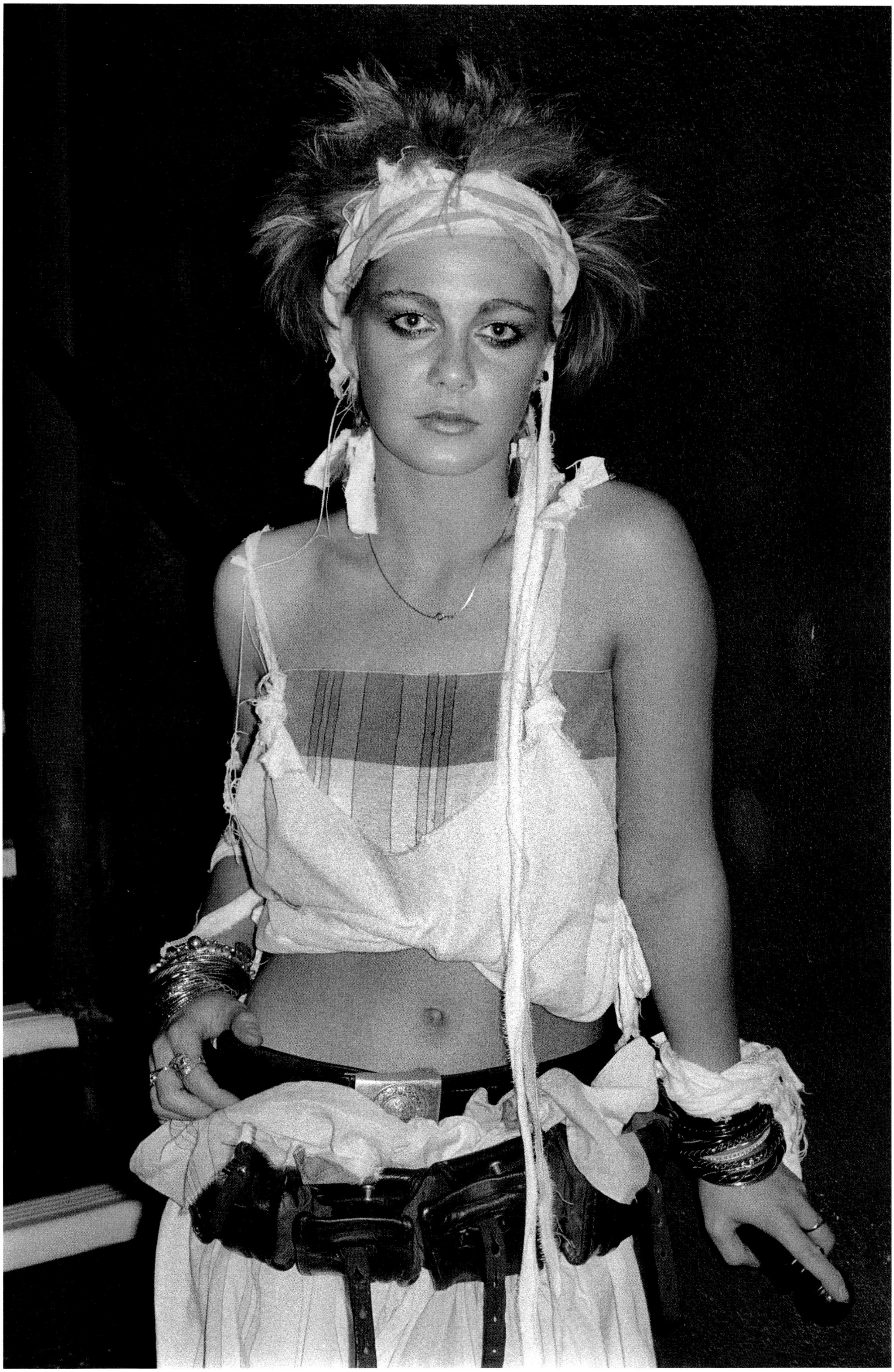

Spit, Soho 1982

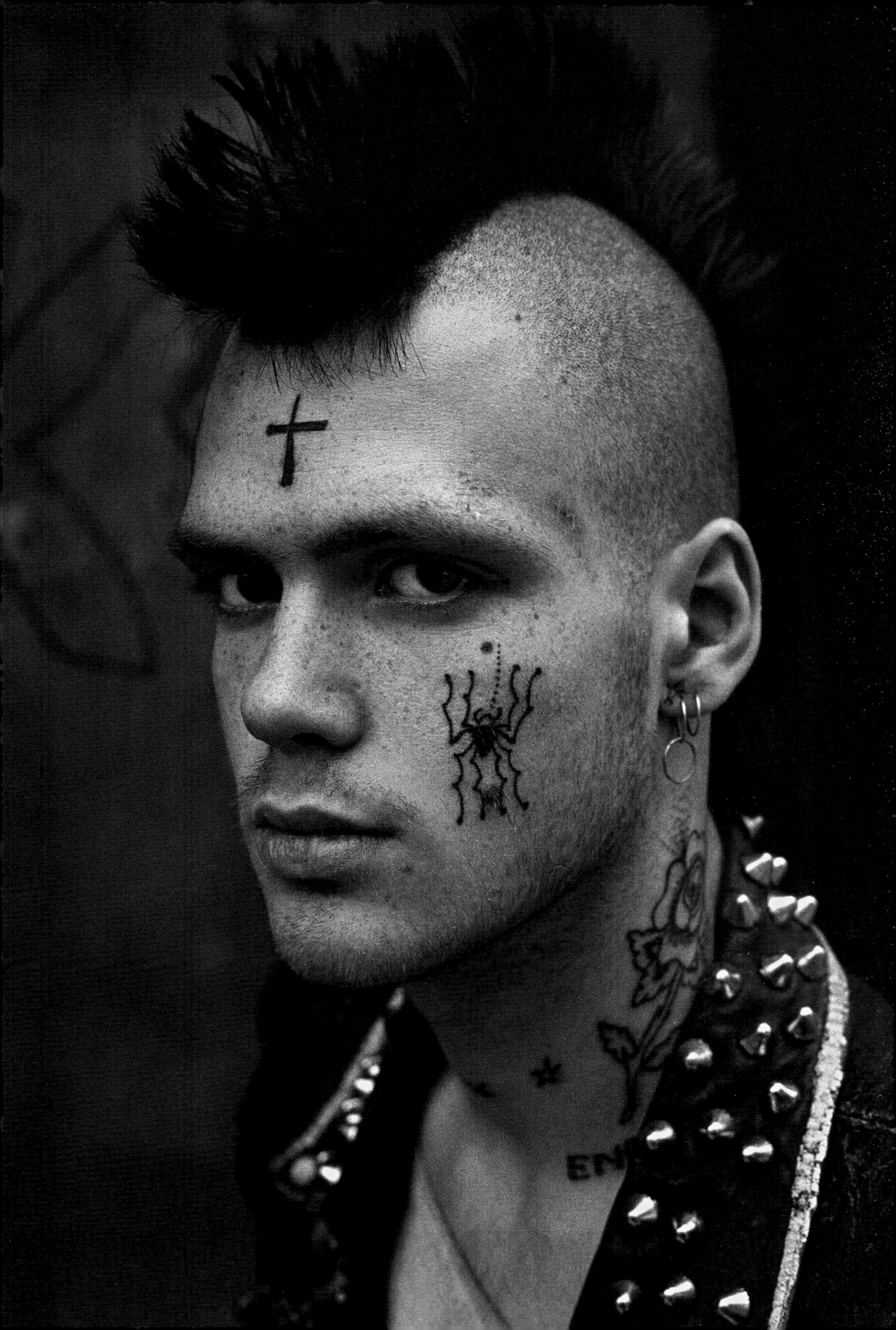

Nicola, Taboo, Leicester Square 1985.

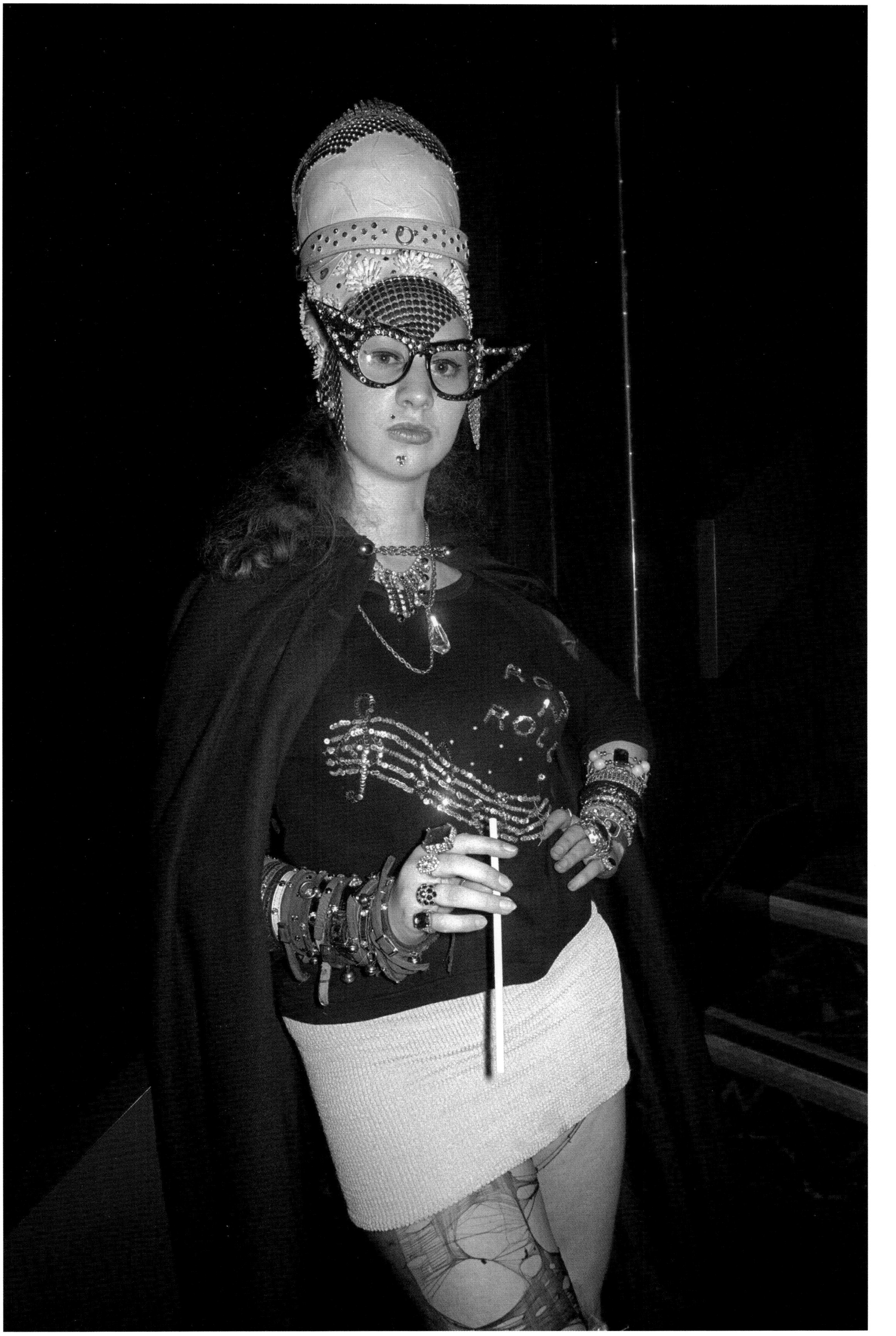

Spike, Brixton 1984.

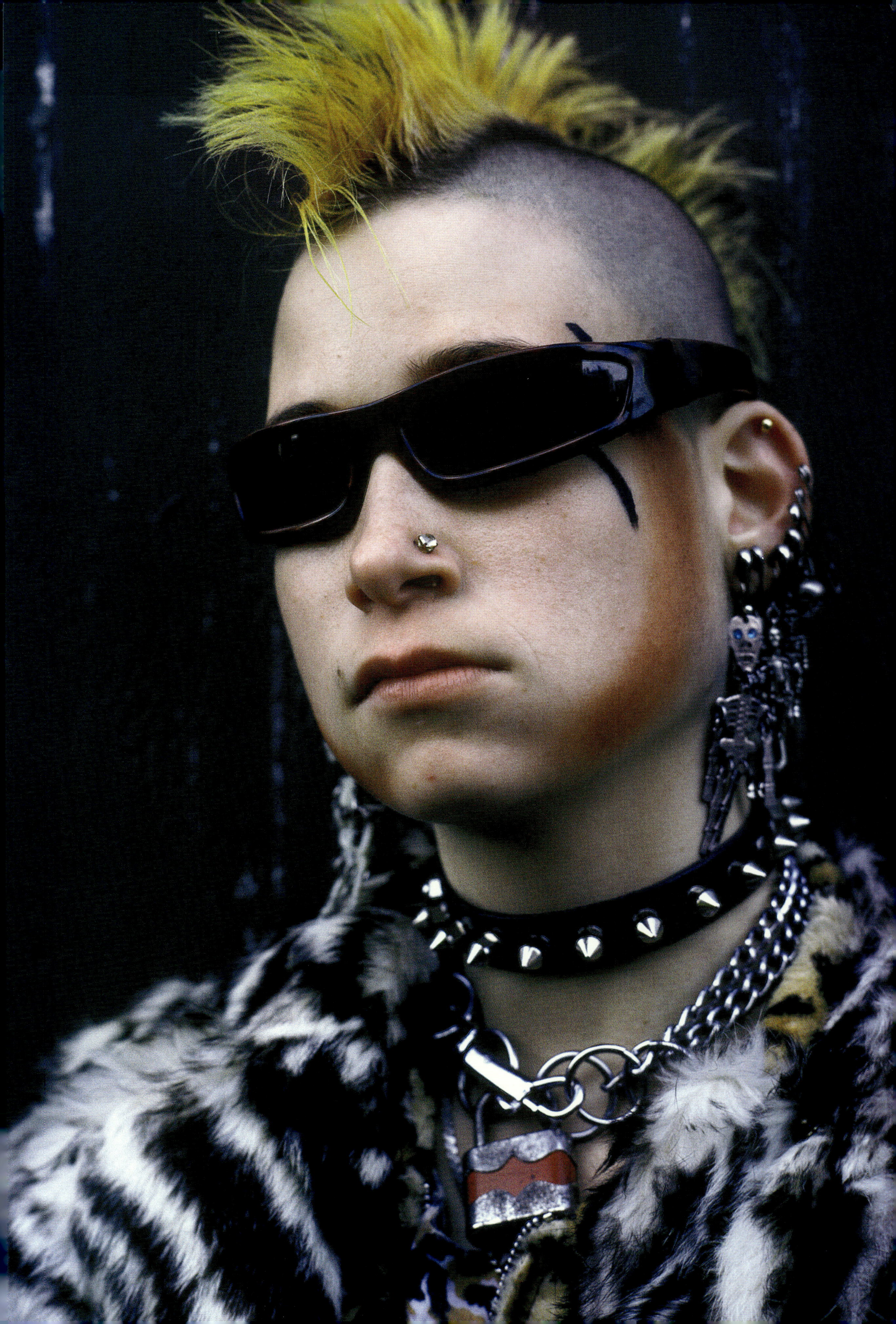

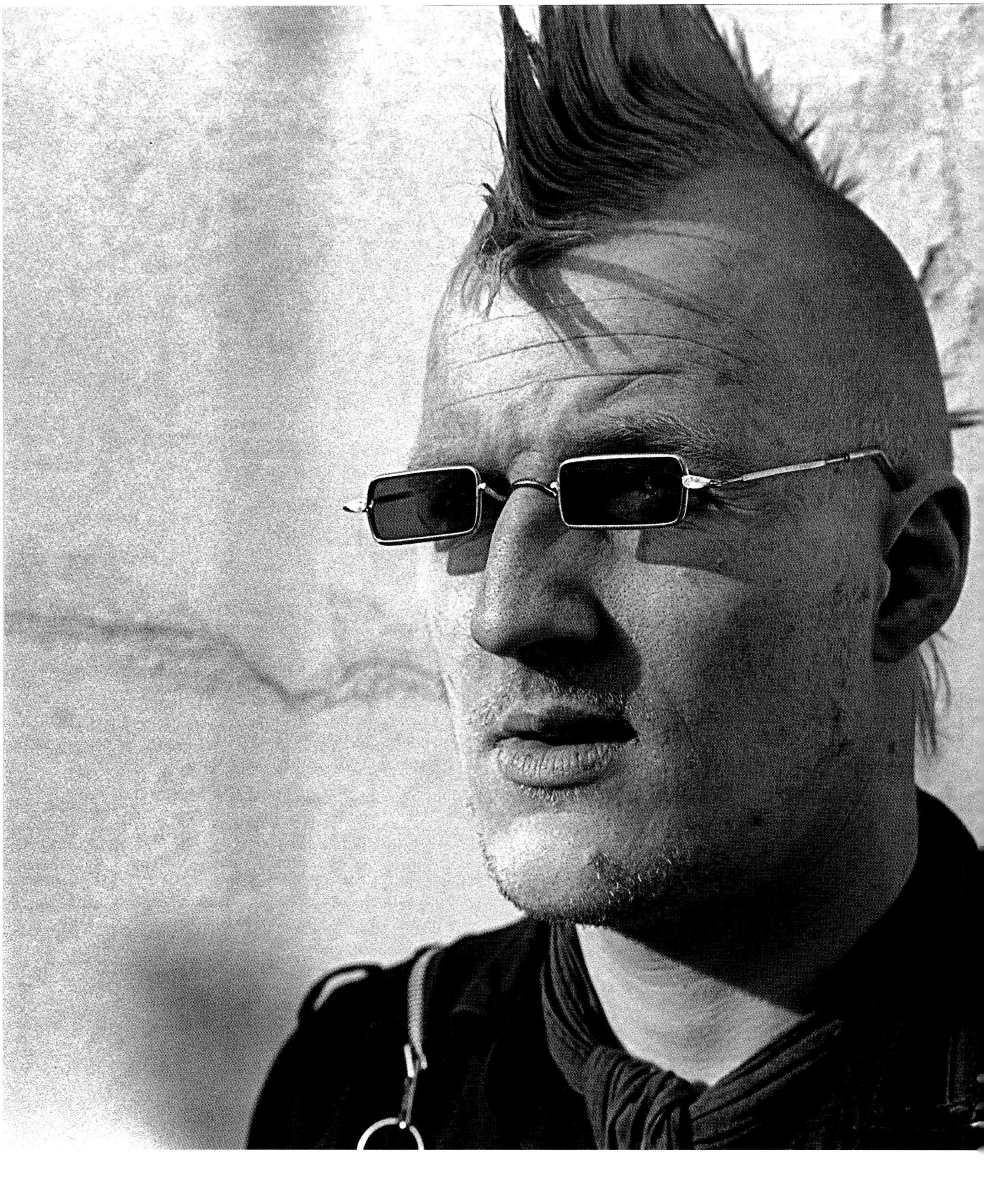

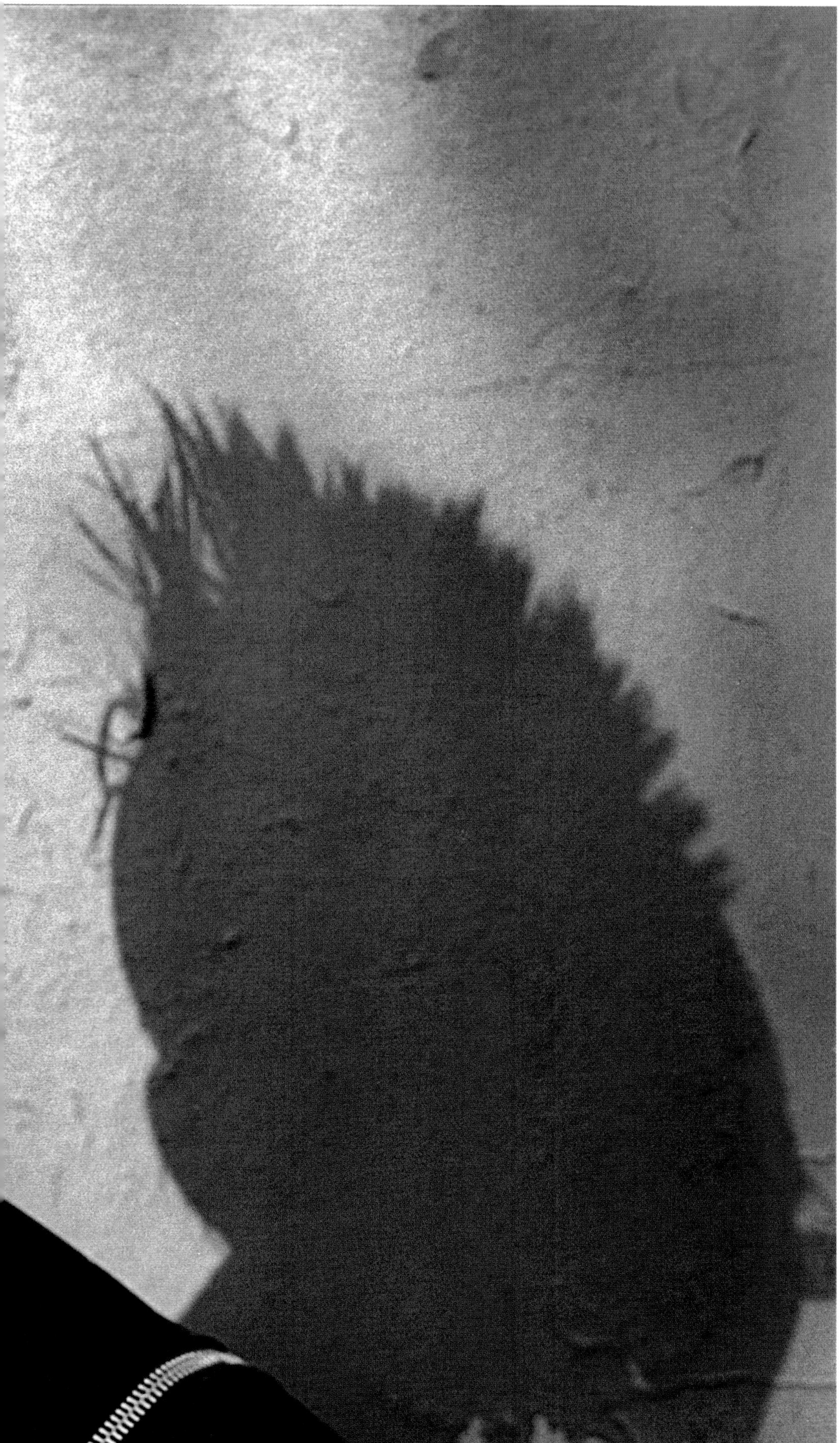

Sniper, Chelsea
1982.

Helen, Carnaby Street 1987.

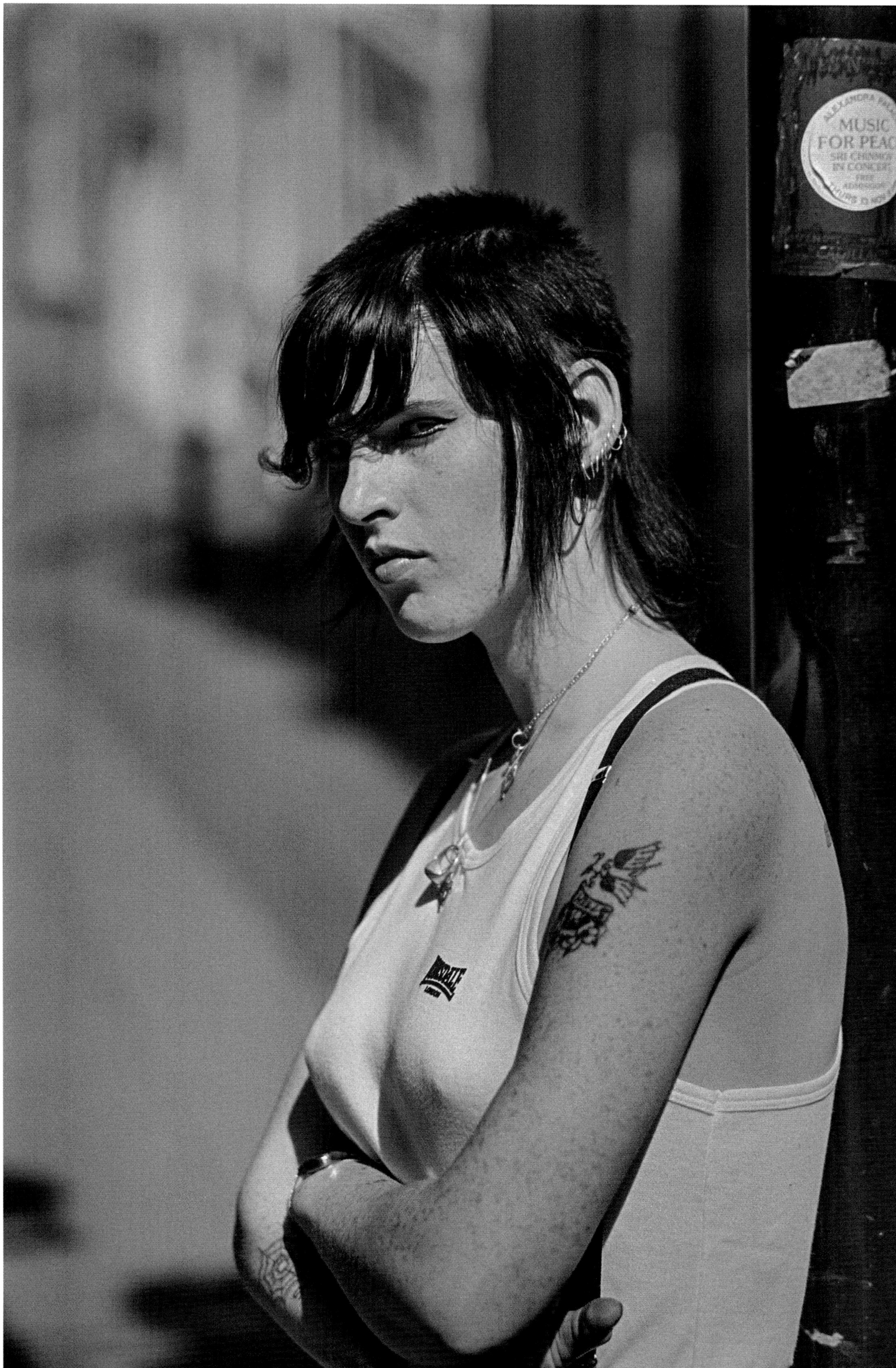
MUSIC
FOR PEACE
SRI CHINMOY
IN CONCERT

Chilo & Kirsty, Shak at Spats, Oxford Street 1987.

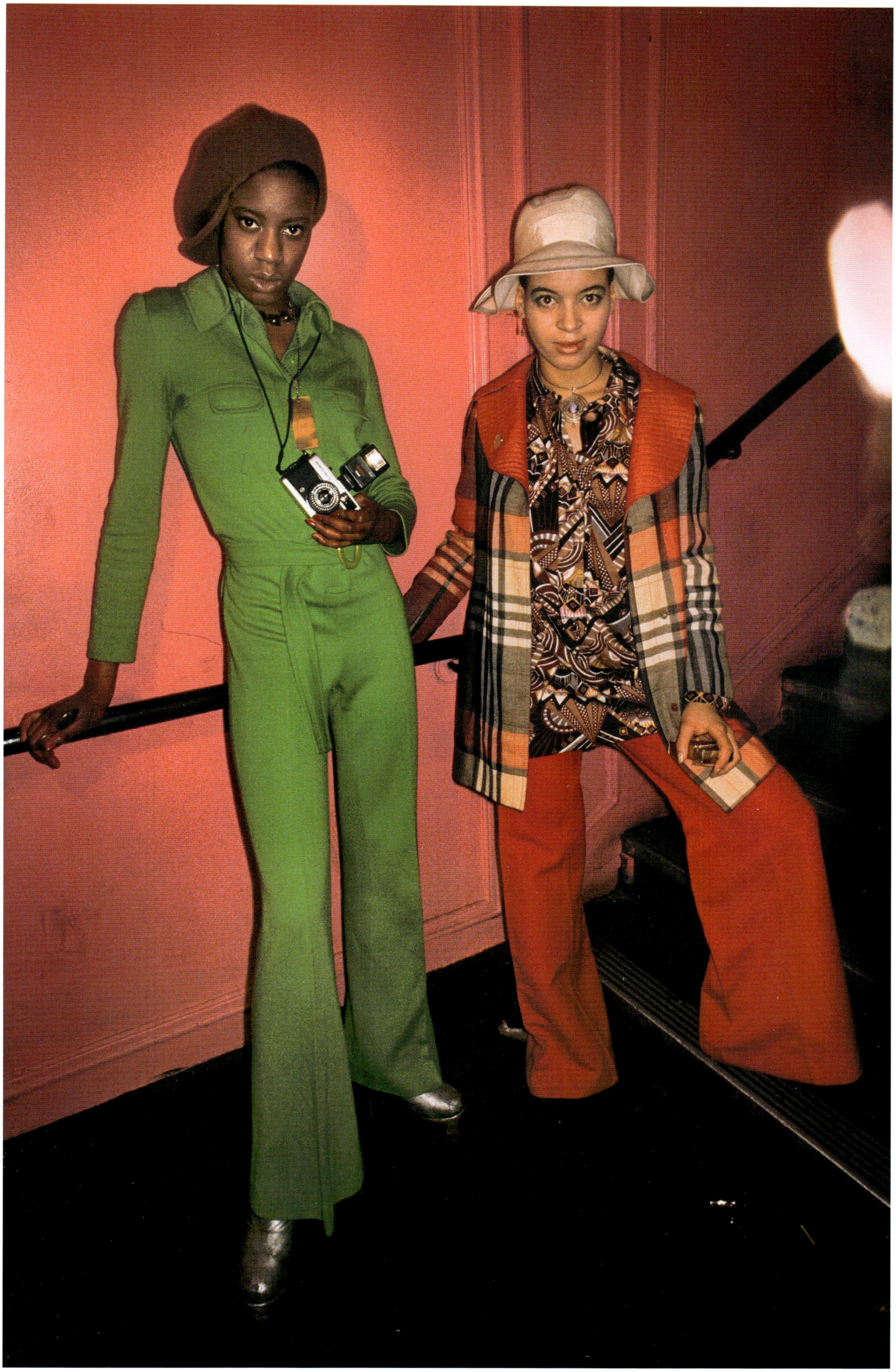

Name unknown, King's Road, Chelsea 1987.

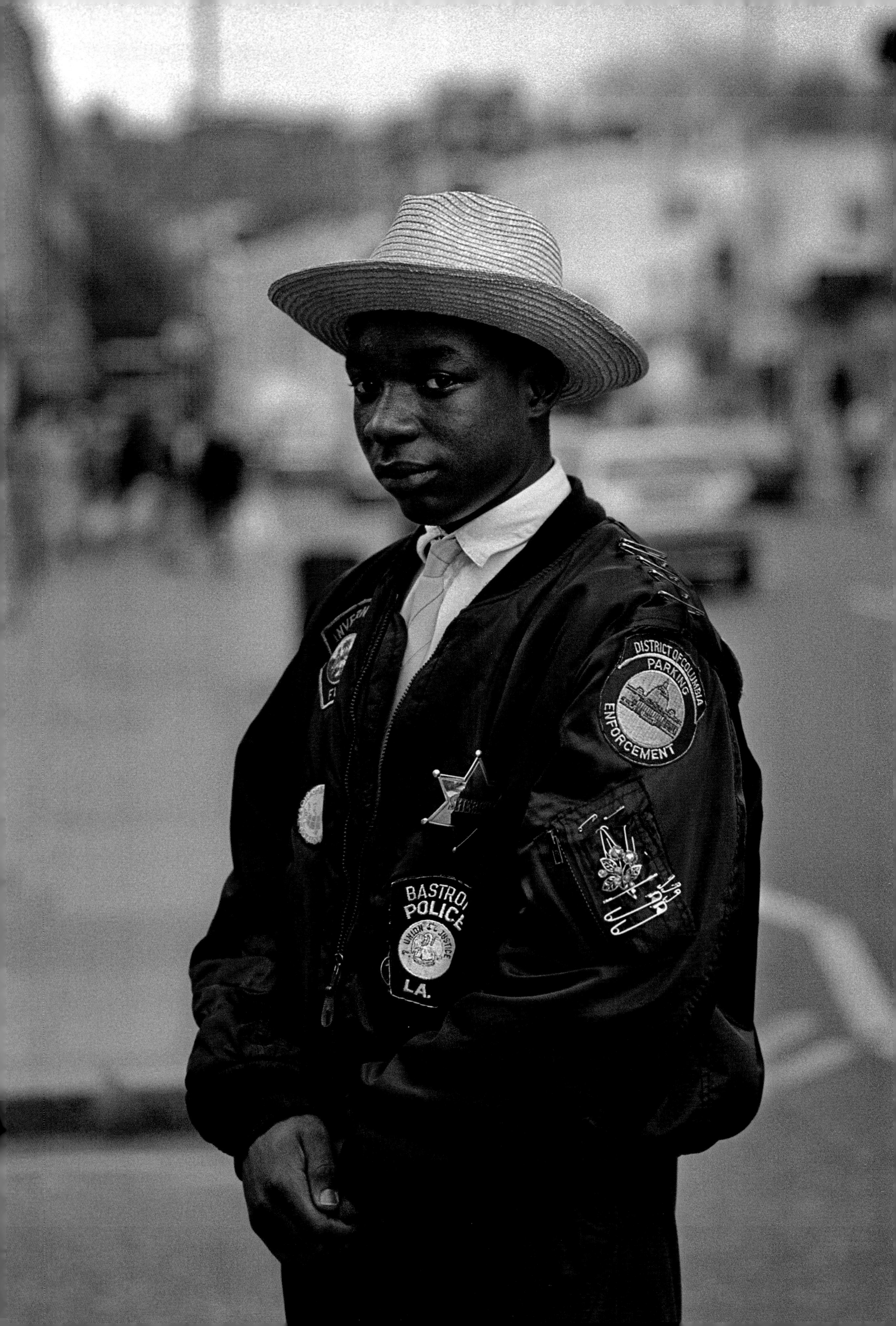
DISTRICT OF COLUMBIA
PARKING
ENFORCEMENT
BASTRO
POLICE
UNION JUSTICE
LA.

Regine, Zeetas, Putney 1986.

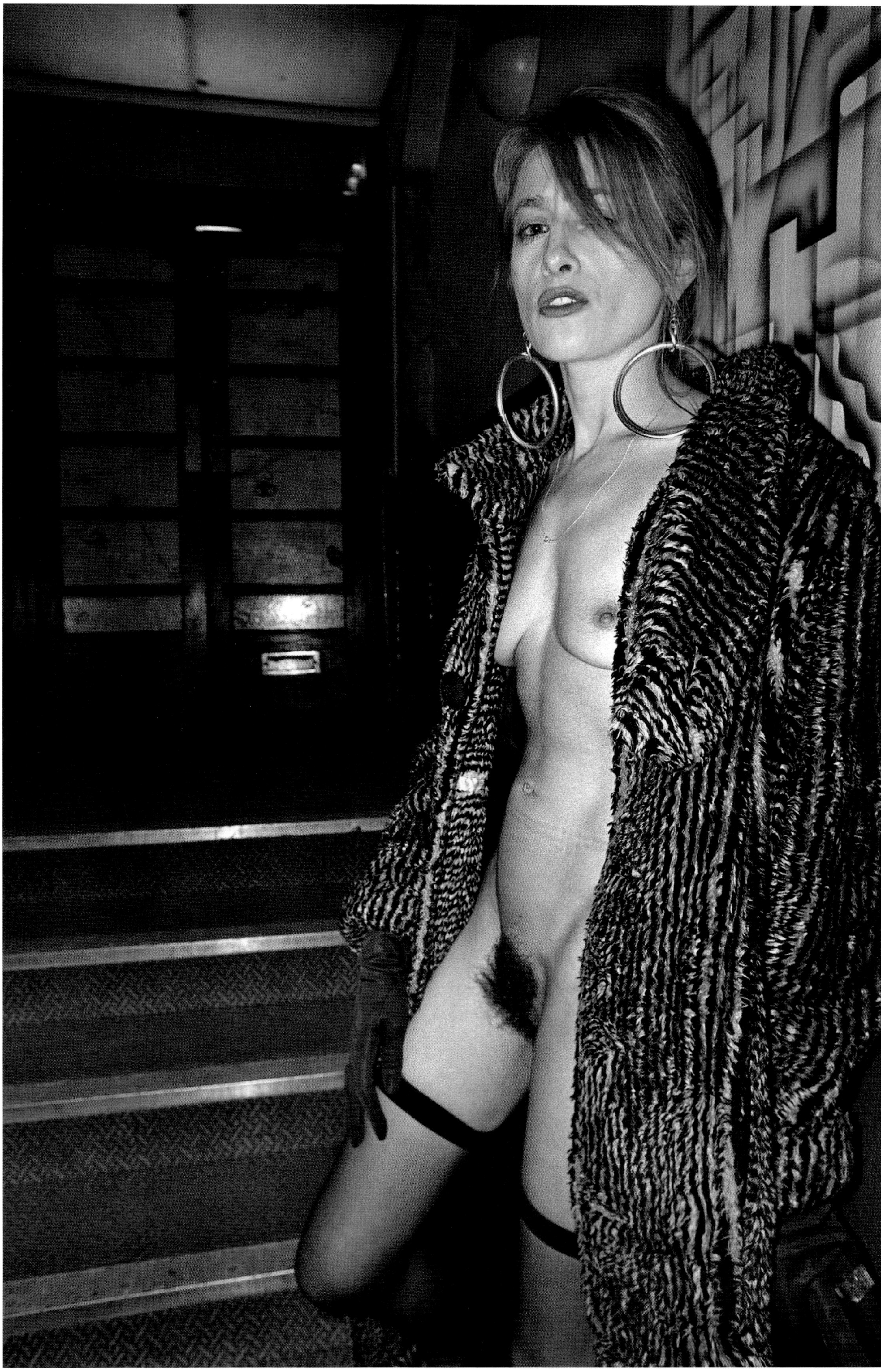

Yolanda, Planets, Mayfair 1983.

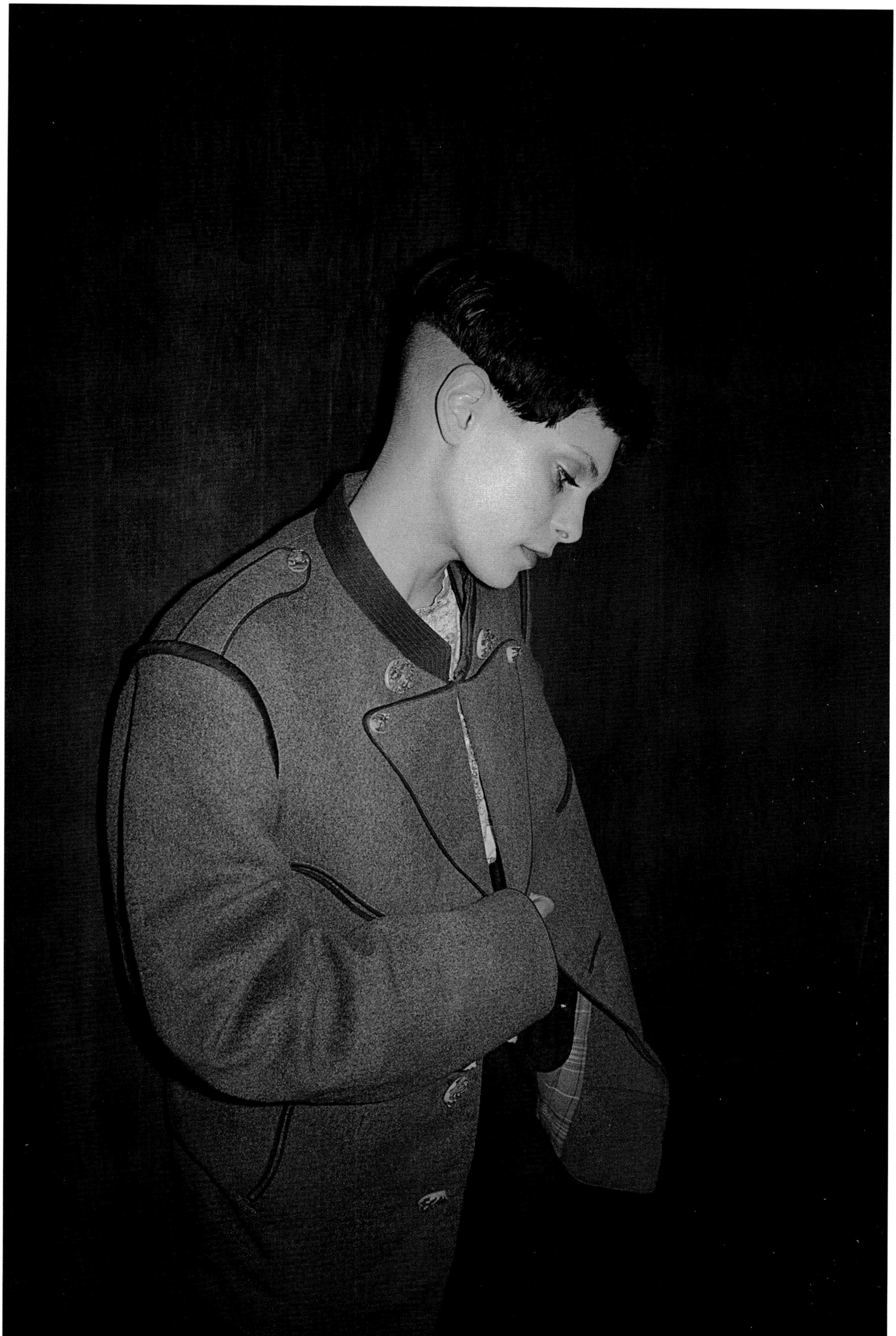

Front cover: *Tuinol Barry*, King's Road, Chelsea 1983. (see p.31)
Page 1: *Babs*, Soho 1987.
Page 3: *Judith*, Batcave 1984.
Page 5: *Perri*, outside Hell, Covent Garden 1980.

This book is dedicated to my wife, Jo-Anne.

I would also like to thank -

Andrea Albertini, Sarah Appelhans, Don Ateyo, Tony Biner, James Brown, Alex Brunner, Andrew Bunney, David Chandler, Sue Compo, Sue Davies, Robin Derrick, Faye Dowling, Jane Garcia, Marcus Georgio, Sue Goodacre, Kasper de Graaf, John Halsall, Mary Harron, Angela Hay, Andrew Heard, Laeticia Hecht, Angela Hill, Fatima Ingraham, Michele Jaffe-Pearce, David Johnson, Carrie Kania, Sarah Kent, Hilaneh von Kories, Babette Kulik, Rae Lewis, Nick Logan, Victoria Lukens, Celia Lunsford, Gordon MacDonald, Lynda Marshall, Peter Marshall, Sean O'Hagan, David Owen, Eleonora Pasqui, Sue Ready, Dany Ridgers, David Robillard, Cynthia Rose, Red Saunders, Jack Schofield, Gary Shove, James Smith, Rupert Smyth, Ava Stander, Tony Stewart, Liz Tray and Professor Val Williams.

ISBN standard edition: 978-1-78884-253-2
ISBN limited edition: 978-1-78884-270-9

A CIP catalogue record for this book is available from the British Library

MIX
Paper | Supporting responsible forestry
FSC® C015829
www.fsc.org

Printed in Italy
for ACC Art Books Ltd., Woodbridge, Suffolk, UK

www.accartbooks.com

ACC ART BOOKS